Truth Is Subjectivity

Robert L. Perkins

TRUTH IS SUBJECTIVITY

Kierkegaard and Political Theology

A SYMPOSIUM IN HONOR OF

ROBERT L. PERKINS

Edited by Sylvia Walsh Perkins

MERCER UNIVERSITY PRESS
Macon, Georgia
1979–2019
40 Years of Publishing Excellence

MUP/ P595

Published by Mercer University Press
1501 Mercer University Drive
Macon, Georgia 31207

9 8 7 6 5 4 3 2 1

Books published by Mercer University Press are printed on acid-free paper that meets the requirements of the American National Standard for Information Sciences—Permanence of Paper for Printed Library Materials.

Printed and bound in the United States.

This book is set in Adobe Caslon Pro.

ISBN 978-0-88146-729-1
Cataloging-in-Publication Data is available from the Library of Congress

Contents

In Memoriam

Robert Lee Perkins

23 June 1930 – 20 March 2018

ABBREVIATIONS

BA *The Book on Adler*, ed. and trans. Howard V. Hong and Edna H. Hong. Princeton: Princeton University Press, 1995.

CA *The Concept of Anxiety*, ed. and trans. Reidar Thomte in collaboration with Albert B. Anderson. Princeton: Princeton University Press, 1980.

CD *Christian Discourses* and *The Crisis and a Crisis in the Life of an Actress*, ed. and trans. Howard V. Hong and Edna H. Hong. Princeton: Princeton University Press, 1997.

CI *The Concept of Irony* together with "Notes on Schelling's Berlin NSBL Lectures," ed. and trans. Howard V. Hong and Edna H. Hong. Princeton: Princeton University Press,1989.

CUP *Concluding Unscientific Postscript to 'Philosophical Fragments,'* 2 vols. ed. and trans. Howard V. Hong and Edna H. Hong. Princeton: Princeton University Press, 1992.

Concluding Unscientific Postscript to the Philosophical Crumbs, ed. and trans. Alastair Hannay (Cambridge: Cambridge University Press, 2009.

COR *The Corsair Affair*, ed. and trans. Howard V. Hong and Edna H. Hong. Princeton University Press, 1982.

DCF *Discourses at the Communion on Fridays*, trans. Sylvia Walsh, Bloomington & Indianapolis: Indiana University Press, 2011.

EO1, 2 *Either/Or*, 2 vols. ed. and trans. Howard V. Hong and Edna H. Hong. Princeton: Princeton University Press, 1987.

EPW *Early Polemical Writings*, ed. and trans. Julia Watkin. Princeton: Princeton University Press, 1990.

EUD *Eighteen Upbuilding Discourses*, ed. and trans. Howard H. Hong and Edna H. Hong. Princeton: Princeton University Press, 1990.

FPOSL *From the Papers of One Still Living*. See *Early Polemical Writings*.

FSE/JFY *For Self-Examination* and *Judge for Yourself!*, ed. and trans. Howard V. Hong and Edna H. Hong. Princeton: Princeton University Press, 1990.

FT *Fear and Trembling*, ed. C. Stephen Evans and Sylvia Walsh and trans. Sylvia Walsh, Cambridge: Cambridge University Press, 2006.

Fear and Trembling and *Repetition*, ed. and trans. Howard V. Hong and Edna H. Hong. Princeton: Princeton University Press, 1983.

Fear and Trembling, trans. Alastair Hannay, London: Penguin Books, 1985.

JC "Johannes Climacus or De omnibus dubitandum est," See *Philosophical Fragments*.

JFY *Judge for Yourself!* See *For Self-Examination*.

JP *Søren Kierkegaard's Journals and Papers*, 7 vols. ed. and trans. Howard V. Hong and Edna H. Hong, assisted by Gregor Malantschuk. Bloomington and London: Indiana University Press, 1, 1967; 2, 1970; 3 and 4, 1975; 5, 1978; 6, 1978; 7, 1978.

KJN *Kierkegaard's Journals and Notebooks*, gen. ed. Bruce H. Kirmmse. Princeton and Oxford: Princeton University Press, 1, 2007; 2, 2008; 3, 2010; 4 and 5, 2011; 6, 2012; 7, 2014; 8, 2015.

LD *Letters and Documents,* ed. and trans. Henrik Rosenmeier. Princeton: Princeton University Press, 1978.

NE *Nicomachean Ethics* in *The Complete Works of Aristotle,* Vol. 2, ed. Jonathan Barnes (Princeton: Princeton University Press, 1995).

PC *Practice in Christianity*, ed. and trans. Howard V. Hong and Edna H. Hong. Princeton: Princeton University Press, 1991.

PCCP *Philosophical Crumbs or A Crumb of Philosophy*, trans. M. G. Piety. Oxford: Oxford University Press, 2009.

PF *Philosophical Fragments* and "Johannes Climacus," ed. and trans. Howard V. Hong and Edna H. Hong. Princeton: Princeton University Press, 1985.

PV, OMWA, AN

The Point of View, "The Single Individual," *On My Work as an Author*, "Armed Neutrality," ed. and trans. Howard V. Hong and Edna H. Hong. Princeton: Princeton University Press, 1998.

R *Repetition*, trans. M. G. Piety. Oxford: Oxford University Press, 2009.

SKP *Søren Kierkegaards Papirer*, 2nd enlarged ed., ed. by Niels Thulstrup, with index vols. 14-16 by Niels Jørgen Cappelørn. Copenhagen: Gyldendal, 1968-78.

SKS *Søren Kierkegaards Skrifter*, ed. Niels Jørgen Cappelørn, Joakim Garff, Jette Knudsen, Johnny Kondrup, and Alastair McKinnon. Published by Søren Kierkegaard Forskningscenteret. Copenhagen: Gads Forlag, 1997-2011.

SLW *Stages on Life's Way*, ed. and trans. Howard V. Hong and Edna H. Hong. Princeton: Princeton University Press, 1988.

SUD *The Sickness unto Death*, ed. and trans. Howard V. Hong and Edna H. Hong. Princeton: Princeton University Press, 1980.

TA *Two Ages: The Age of Revolution and The Present Age. A Literary Review*, ed. and trans. Howard V. Hong and Edna H. Hong. Princeton: Princeton University Press, 1978.

TDIO *Three Discourses on Imagined Occasions*, ed. and trans. Howard V. Hong and Edna H. Hong. Princeton: Princeton University Press, 1993.

TM *'The Moment' and Late Writings*, ed. and trans. Howard V. Hong and Edna H. Hong. Princeton: Princeton University Press, 1998.

UDVS *Upbuilding Discourses in Various Spirits*, ed. and trans. Howard V. Hong and Edna H. Hong. Princeton: Princeton University Press, 1993.

WA *Without Authority*, ed. and trans. Howard V. Hong and Edna H. Hong. Princeton: Princeton University Press, 1997.

WL *Works of Love*, ed. and trans. Howard V. Hong and Edna H. Hong. Princeton: Princeton University Press, 1995.

MERCER UNIVERSITY

MERCER UNIVERSITY PRESS

Endowed by

TOM WATSON BROWN

and

THE WATSON-BROWN FOUNDATION, INC.

Foreword

A Tribute to Robert Lee Perkins

The study of existential philosophy is meant—I suppose—to prepare you for life's tumult. I suppose, but existence being what it is, that isn't always the case.

I received the news about Bob's death at a conference in Berkeley, and found myself hauled up and out of the hustle of watching the clock and fielding questions. The passage of someone you care about causes an eerie pause: things felt shorn, deracinated, and the ordinary now extraordinarily empty. The worn saying "when a person dies, an encyclopedia goes out of existence" came uncomfortably to mind. But of course nothing actually does pause, and thus I found myself on the phone with Bob's fellow Kierkegaard scholar and spouse, Sylvia Walsh; perhaps the first sensible sentence I uttered was "we must have a panel in Bob's honor." And what better venue to celebrate Bob's life and work than at a session of the Søren Kierkegaard Society, an organization that he founded in 1978? We went to work assembling a remarkable panel of speakers (you will hear more about their contributions in the Introduction). The session itself, held at the American Academy of Religion meeting on November 17, 2018, was riveting—not a word I'm accustomed to using in connection with academic presentations—and those assembled agreed that a volume was clearly in order.

Bob's extensive contribution to Kierkegaard scholarship is, of course, well known and widely celebrated. What you may not know is that Bob was committed to mentoring those just entering Kierkegaard's fearsome terrain. Many academics who now traverse Kierkegaardiana with ease were first encouraged by Bob: his criticisms, and praise, were crafted to meet the author where she or he was, and designed to bring that thinker into the wider conversation. Bob's careful concern for his fellow Kierkegaardians bespeaks values that are central to the existential enterprise: the careful scrutiny of one's subjective condition and a commitment to the social and civic order are always in the foreground. Both Bob and Sylvia have dedicated their professional and personal lives to the utterly Kierkegaardian pursuit of intersubjective social justice, and to the deep reality that truth is indeed subjectivity.

Please enjoy these marvelously thoughtful and inspiring essays. Yes, losing Bob was indeed to lose his encyclopedia—thank goodness that many, many of those pages have been carefully and lovingly annotated. Professor Robert Lee Perkins's passions and projects live on.

—Sheridan Hough
President, Søren Kierkegaard Society

INTRODUCTION

The essays that make up this volume were originally presented at a Symposium in Honor of Robert L. Perkins at the annual meeting of the Søren Kierkegaard Society in Denver, Colorado, in 2018. As most if not all Kierkegaard scholars are aware, Dr. Perkins was the General Editor of the twenty-four volume *International Kierkegaard Commentary* published by Mercer University Press. What many scholars may not know, however, is that he was also the founder of the Søren Kierkegaard Society in North America as well as the *Kierkegaard Newsletter*. It was therefore especially appropriate for the Søren Kierkegaard Society to remember and honor him upon his recent passing. While serving as Professor and Chair of the Department of Philosophy at the University of South Alabama and later as Dean of the College of Arts and Sciences, Professor and Chair of the Department of Philosophy, Professor Emeritus, and Senior Research Scholar at Stetson University, Dr. Perkins also published many articles on Kierkegaard, especially on Kierkegaard's social and political thought. Focusing on an aspect of Kierkegaard's writings that had been relatively neglected in studies of his thought, Dr. Perkins was both a leader and a promoter of scholarship on this topic. The present essays generated so much interest and discussion at the symposium that it was widely agreed upon that they should be published, which Mercer University Press has graciously consented to do in honor of Dr.

Perkins. By making these essays accessible to a wider audience, it is hoped that they will continue to generate an ongoing interest in, and focus on, this aspect of Kierkegaard's thought among both established and new Kierkegaard scholars and readers. Toward that end, a Select Bibliography of other studies relating to this topic is included in the volume.

The essays in this volume cover a wide range of viewpoints and aspects of Kierkegaard's understanding and attitude toward the political dimension of human life.

Focusing on what he identifies as the central paradox in Kierkegaard's political theology, namely the God-given potential of every person to manifest Christian love towards others even in the context of material circumstances that can diminish or embitter one's belief in one's potential to do so, John Davenport argues in agreement with Perkins that we can and should pursue finite goals in our social life, including political initiatives. Noting changes in Kierkegaard's views toward the political over the course of his authorship, particularly his critique of that realm, Davenport applies Kierkegaard's critique to the political factions of the present time, both the left and the right, and comes to the conclusion that while Kierkegaard's political critique is correct, it focuses too little on the leaders who shape trends in mass culture.

Noting the apocryphal (concealed) as well as equivocal meaning of politics as that term applies to Kierkegaard, M.G. Piety focuses on Kierkegaard's expressly held conservative, monarchal political views in distinction from those that may be inferred from or cohere with his general philosophical and theological views. She contends that the former do not stem from any sort of social elitism or contempt for the public good on his part but rather from his contempt for the mob and his cynicism concerning the ability of large groups of people to govern themselves in a humane fashion. Only by properly relating ourselves to God is it possible to properly understand and relate ourselves to others in Christian love of the neighbor. Like Plato, who in the *Republic* contends that a proper relation to the Good and genuine knowledge of justice require a conversion within the individual, the same can be said of Kierkegaard, whose primary concern was always the spiritual situation of the individual.

C. Stephen Evans also notes Kierkegaard's lack of interest in politics as such, which contra Hegel was regarded as relative and temporally contingent rather than absolute and eternal. Focusing on the logical political implications of Kierkegaard's most significant concepts, namely his view of human equality and the duty to love, Evans contends that while these concepts do not depend on contingent factors for Kierkegaard, they are nevertheless applicable to and important for the historical realm even though perfect equality is not realizable in human society. As examples, he points to Kierkegaard's approval of the abolition of slavery, feudalism, and inhumane treatment of women while also recognizing the limitations of Kierkegaard's personal view concerning the emancipation of women.

Taking his cue from Hannah Arendt's reflections on politics and political action, George Pattison emphasizes the political nature of speech as the primary form of political expression by Kierkegaard. Pattison focuses on the urbanity or urbane character of Kierkegaard's writings in both his pseudonymous and signed works in adopting the pose of a "flâneur" or sophisticated, idle, piquant, esthetic, urbane individual who participates as a citizen in political life at a distance in the form of political discourse in the character of an author rather than as a Christian witness or disciple in the imitation of Jesus Christ in the expression of Christian love.

Briefly summarizing the variety of interpretations of Kierkegaard's politics, including liberal, conservative, anti-elitist, anti-totalitarian, anti-traditionalist, anti-political, and anti-nationalist interpretations, Lee Barrett follows Robert Perkins in finding clues of Kierkegaard's political sensibilities in his exposition of Christian love of the neighbor, and in addressing the question of whether there is a political dimension to this command in determining what it means to build up love in others as expressed in *Works of Love*. Barrett emphasizes the multi-layered and multivocal character of this work in the process of laying out the societal dynamics in it, pointing out the limitations and obstacles as well as the possibilities of political action that support the upbuilding of love in others.

Beginning and ending with an account of his own personal correspondence with Robert Perkins on the political dimension of Kierkegaard's works, Christopher A. P. Nelson both sums up and raises some important questions with respect to each of the previous essays. He ends with an indication of how they have helped him come to terms in particular with the concept of "capability communication" in Kierkegaard's thought, which may be understood as involving not only the capacity to love but also, and perhaps especially, the capacity of being willing to be unconditionally loved by others.

With this bird's eye view of what is ahead, the reader is now invited to read, absorb, and critique the insights that are presented by the contributors to this volume. Hopefully she or he will be led to join and extend the conversation with Kierkegaard on this important question concerning the role of the political in human life.

The Crowd and Populism: The Insights and Limits of Kierkegaard on the Profanity of Politics

John J. Davenport

I. The Problem: A Paradox of Inward Love and External Goods

This essay is inspired by the life-work of Robert L. Perkins, who argued that Kierkegaard had much of value to contribute to thinking about social and political life, broadly understood. In an essay in Martin Matuštik's and Merold Westphal's collection, which highlighted both Kierkegaard's political relevance and the way his themes challenge our ordinary sense of social identity, Bob helpfully compared Kierkegaard to Martin Buber, who argued that aesthetic egoism was spiritually harmful and defended the need for living dialogical relations between persons as unique individuals.[1] Bob rightly recognized that in an era of increasingly tribal

---

[1] See Robert Perkins, "The Politics of Existence: Buber and Kierkegaard," in *Kierkegaard in Post/Modernity*, ed. Martin Matuštik and Merold Westphal (Indiana Univ. Press, 1995): 167-81. Bob's essay immediately precedes Habermas's essay in the same volume.

politics that exploits people's senses of group identity,[2] we may benefit from Kierkegaard's critique of politics.

This critique is not easy to construe in its most defensible form, because Kierkegaard gave us a metaethical account of neighbor-love as a kind of motive without enough normative content to link agape with justice in "secular" affairs. Unlike Augustine, who at least indirectly influenced Kierkegaard, it was never one of his main tasks to defend sets of ethical principles to cover the main domains of human activity, from war and politics to civil society and domestic improvements. He was instead focused on the "how"—that is, our attitudes towards our responsibilities and relationships in these domains, and the ways we address them, as governed by the God-relationship that transcends them. This leaves us with the problem that Kierkegaard can easily appear simply to be advocating pietist withdrawal from all temporal affairs or social life, despite his insistence that a Christian must challenge secular betrayals of humanity—"the tendency of every Established order to deify itself"—even at the risk of great personal suffering.[3] This quietist interpretation of Kierkegaard is the basis of dismissals like Karl Mannheim's, which Bob Perkins worked so hard to correct.[4]

To avoid this, we have to make sense of the central "paradox" addressed by Lee Barrett, George Pattison, and others in this collection, namely, that every single person has the same innate God-

---

[2] See, for ex., Amy Chua, "Tribal World: Group Identity is All," *Foreign Affairs* (July/August, 2018): 25-33.

[3] See Merold Westphal, *Kierkegaard's Concept of Faith* (Wm. B. Eerdmans, 2014) 270-1, and Wetsphal, "Kierkegaard's Religiousness C: A Defense," *International Philosophical Quarterly*, 44 np.4 (2004): 535-48. Also see Sylvia Walsh, *Kierkegaard and Religion: Personality, Character, and Virtue* (Cambridge University Press, 2018), esp. chs. 4-5.

[4] Perkins, "The Politics of Existence: Buber and Kierkegaard," p.181 N.14.

given potential for agapic love, which their external circumstances in the world cannot erase—even though we know from experience that great material hardship and oppression can embitter people or even, in extreme cases, diminish their very ability to believe in their own agency or positive potential. This is why, for example, restorative justice is so important in criminal justice contexts: it can help convicts rediscover their true capacity to do good and to be loving persons. Kierkegaard often, though not always, minimizes the second half of this paradox, because he holds that Christianity must focus on that inner *constitutive level* at which eternal equality holds, and where life-meaning can be found through agapic loving no matter what finite, earthly goods one can achieve or has materially at one's disposal.

There are two parts to this theme throughout Kierkegaard's explicitly Christian works. First, the *purity thesis* holds that the highest form of ethical willing depends on loving others for their own sake beyond any concern for one's own finite goods or without conditioning love on receiving reciprocation. "Dying to the world" corresponds in the explicitly Christian works to "infinite resignation" in *Fear and Trembling* and the *Postscript*: it is the transition necessary before the movement (or reception) of faith in the strict sense is possible (FSE 81-83). "Dying" in this sense purifies our motives of any dependency on external success or material achievements. Second, the *inwardness thesis* insists that what matters for a person's spiritual development is this pure quality of their volitional motives, which can be maintained without external reward, rather than any outward achievements which may depend on material resources. These ideas, which are especially pronounced in *Works of Love*, *Upbuilding Discourses in Various Spirits*, and other late works, are analogous to Kant's notion of moral worth residing in the good will; the difference is that strictly, for Christianity, we can never attribute moral worth to ourselves.[5]

In sympathy with Perkins' project, I will argue that these theses are compatible with insisting that we can (and most people should) seriously pursue important finite goods in social life, even including political initiatives. Given that being loved by others helps upbuild people to love in turn, alleviating great injustices may also reduce certain contingent obstacles to cultivating neighbor-love, such as causes of resentment, extreme depression, and disabling loss of self-respect. This *justice thesis* points to general obstacles with effects that vary widely by circumstance; for Kierkegaard was surely correct both that people in the most terrible circumstances have sometimes shown miraculous neighbor-love, and that improvements in people's financial state or social status may instead facilitate their corruption. We know, for example, that winning a large lottery has sometimes led people to destroy all their social relationships and ruin their lives. Moreover, Kierkegaard pointed to more regular and predictable corrupting effects of certain kinds of social and political movements that degrade people's authenticity, reduce their ethical concerns to aesthetic posturing, and encourage them towards arrogance and hatred of other groups. I will argue below that this *profanity thesis* about politics contains crucial insights that apply quite profoundly to the current American situation: thus it should be retained within a

[5] See my accounts of the relation between neighbor-love and the special loves in Davenport, "The Integration of Neighbor-Love and the Special Loves in Kierkegaard and von Hildebrand," in *Kierkegaard's God and the Good Life*, ed. J. Aaron Simmons and Michael Strawser (Indiana University Press, 2017): 46-77; and "The Esthetic Validity of Marriage: Romantic Marriage as a Model for Ethical Will—A Defense of Judge Wilhelm," in the Klassiker Auslegen volume on *Søren Kierkegaard: Entweder-Oder [Either/Or]*, ed. Hermann Deuser and Markus Kleinert (Walter de Gruyter, 2017): 169-91.

charitable contemporary reconstruction of Kierkegaard's position that combines his best points so as to address the paradox. Notably, recognition that some kinds of political movements are a threat to authentic faith actually *confirms* the justice thesis, while cautioning that collective efforts to address injustice need to avoid methods that involve profanizing forms of mass consciousness.

However, this reconstruction of the most defensible Kierkegaardian view, which I can only sketch in this essay, should reject Kierkegaard's occasional implications—especially in his late work after 1848—that the most ideal or rigorous Christian life should spurn all engagement in legal and social reform efforts, or even meritocratic social processes.[6] For political projects need not encourage aestheticism; they *can* have an ethical character, even if the danger of self-righteousness is inherent in them. The Christian ideal need not imply that the only direct relation we should have to political causes or movements is a negative one whereby we expose their shallowness, or oppose them all in ways that inevitably lead to martyrdom, if strictly carried through. If the *martyrdom thesis* in Kierkegaard's late works is interpreted this way, it should be set aside in our most charitable reconstruction. While we can never measure a good will by outward success (as per the inwardness thesis), we also cannot measure purity of heart by *lack*

[6] Can a Christian "disdain the world's honor and glory, rank and titles, medals and ribbons," etc. and yet accept honors that come through pursuit of a legitimate career while admitting that spiritually, these are all nothing? It is unclear in *Judge for Yourself*; at least, Kierkegaard mocks those who inauthentically try to add religion to their lives after giving social status priority. He compares this to getting married first and then preaching that Christianity prefers "the single state" (as if a spouse were a status symbol?) (JFY 138-39). When Kierkegaard starts to argue for celibacy and even an antinatalist end to childbirth in his very last writing, he has passed from infinite resignation to a kind of unChristian despair over creation.

of success in bringing about finite goods involved in human justice—that could never be more than a contingent prediction, given that effort and luck sometimes overcome social and political evils.[7]

This does not mean that the ethical demands of Christianity should be toned down to make them more palatable or easily achievable by human effort, as Kierkegaard thought "enlightenment and culture" in his time were saying (JFY 155). We can accept an infinite ethical demand (JYF 154) even while we affirm the justice thesis.[8] Nor does rejecting the martyrdom stance or solely negative relations to political reform movements entail serving "two masters" (JYF 150-52), because the requirements of neighbor-love always transcend and regulate any pursuit of finite ends through political means or other collective action. This ultimate eternal standard can require us to accept failure in such efforts or abandon them when only immoral methods could succeed. Thus we can "give what is Caesar's to Caesar" without serving Caesar (the state, politics, collective initiatives) as our master. In the next section, I canvass several of Kierkegaard's most pithy points on politics to see whether this balanced reconstruction of his position can be made plausible.

II. Kierkegaard's Critique of Politics: A Way towards a Balanced View

While Kierkegaard's negative attitude towards political movements is often blamed on a stubborn cultural conservatism that

---

[7] It was revealed to Christ's disciples that they risked "certain downfall" in the world (CD 184), but we have no comparable basis for this certainty.

[8] As Knud Løgstrup's work continually argued; also see my discussion of Kierkegaard's perfectionist requirement in Davenport, "My *Schindler's List*: A Personal Kierkegaardian Reflection," *Religious Humanism* 34 nos. 2 and 3 (summer/fall 2001): 13-23.

made him doubt the democratic populisms of his period, I will argue instead that the essence of his critique—which stands or falls quite apart from his personal predilections—concerns probable reductions of higher values to *aesthetic* posturing in search of acceptance and status-seeking, i.e. "spiritless" attitudes beneath any robust sense of good and evil.

In Tome V of the valuable *Kierkegaard's Concepts* volumes in the KRSRR series, Leo Stan's very helpful analysis stresses Kierkegaard's worry that "national and communal goals, no matter how selfless," should never be conflated with a relation to God.[9] As Bob Perkins also noted, for Kierkegaard, political efforts are rarely selfless: the state is largely based on egoism and thus tends to promote aesthetic attitudes to life; political activities "threaten religious fulfillment by virtue of its affinity with the numerical and the crowd." For, in democratic politics, everything depends on having numbers on one's side rather than on individual conviction and inner strength in accord with conscience.[10] According to Stan, Kierkegaard valued reason in political matters, even though political institutions cannot reach to the heart of personal life; thus he feared the games and tricks used to gin up crowd movements not motivated by any rational understanding of the issues.[11] These themes are most apparent in Kierkegaard's famous essay on "The Present Age," which argued that the politics of his time prevented an individual's "ethical stance" by encouraging each to wait indecisively on the general trend of thought (TA 106). Thus politics motivated by genuine ethical commitment has declined: people

[9] Leo Stan, "Politics,"in *Kierkegaard's Concepts: Tome V: Objectivity to Sacrifice*, ed. Steven Emmanuel, William Desmond, and Jon Stewart (Ashgate, 2015): 101-5, p.101.

[10] Ibid, p.103. Compare Perkins, "The Politics of Existence," p.176.

[11] Leo Stan, "Politics," pp.104-5. Also see the Preface to Kierkegaard's *Two Ages*.

will either be lost in the aesthetic "dizziness of abstract infinity or be saved infinitely in...the religious life" (TA 108). In this pessimistic view, the ethical "sphere" among Kierkegaard's triad falls out of the realm of civic relationships and legal reform.

In his analysis of Kierkegaard's literary review of *Two Ages*, George Pattison makes a similar point. While Gyllembourg's novel presents both the negatives *and positives* of modern innovations in city life, like the creation of the Tivoli amusement park, Kierkegaard focuses only on the affectation, "smug conceit," vanity, desire to be seen by others as hip, and incapability of taking any ethical stand that flows from the irresistible corrosive spread of aesthetic culture.[12] Pattison thus correctly sees Kierkegaard as following J.L. Heiberg's "assimilation of the aesthetic and the political,"[13] which tends to imply (over-pessimistcally) that ethical motivation will never guide political action.

This critique of aestheticism is just as crucial in the relevant late works as is *Either/Or*. We can see this, for example, in Kierkegaard's discourse on *Matthew* ch.19, which equates "worldliness" with a "sagacity" that can "ingeniously avoid every decision" or ethical commitment (CD 181). Similarly, in "The Care of Indecisiveness" discourse, the point of the Lily and Bird figures to which Kierkegaard so often returned is said to be that they belong "to one master;" whereas they do so instinctively, we must do so by free response (CD 82, 84). The way to purify faith from any dependence on outward success (even in ethically valuable endeavors) is then to cut it from "all connections with the surrounding world" (CD 87)—a version of inwardness test of purity that unfortunately sounds like total withdrawal.

---

[12] George Pattison, *Kierkegaard, Religion, and the Nineteenth-Century Crisis of Culture* (Cambridge University Press, 2002) 50-64.

[13] Ibid, 65.

Thus Kierkegaard's portrayal obscures the difference between *worldliness as aestheticism*—his real concern—and simply pursuing finite goods, which can be done within governance by eternal ideals of neighbor-love. But it helps explain his conviction, restated in his late unpublished essay "Armed Neutrality," that by equating Christianity with an established church and forms of cultural progress celebrated in speculative terms, we have "thrown all Christianity back into the esthetic." This "worldliness" of Christian practices in Denmark consisted not in ordinary human concern for finite ends, but in shifting us away from concrete ethical demands towards "the intellectual, the metaphysical, the imaginational"—as if by partaking in a "theatrical" politics we could fulfill the love-commandments (PV 30).

From this aesthetic view of politics, it was easy for Kierkegaard to slide into formulations implying that the ideal Christian should be neutral on the actual content of political debates: we avoid the fanaticism of self-righteousness only if we are not "finitely polemical against anything finite" (such as current social roles or prevailing customs), and thus do "not lean towards any decision in the external, secular world" (PV 133). Call this the *neutrality thesis*. Kierkegaard explains the title of "Armed Neutrality" as meaning that in Christendom, no one should proclaim themselves to be a Christian, as if they were an exemplary figure whom others could follow (PV 139)—which is the danger seen in fanatical religious "awakeners." But the title could almost equally stand for the political neutrality that Kierkegaard seems to have drawn from the passages in *Matthew* ch.6 on which he wrote so much.

Jesus's apparent political neutrality was clearly Kierkegaard's model here. In his ethical-religious essay on whether we have a right to let ourselves be killed for the truth, Kierkegaard describes the upset that Jesus caused by refusing to lead a national liberation from Roman domination: he was bound "to be an offense to the upper class as well as to the lower class"—to the priests and Pharisees as well as to followers of Simon the Zealot—"since he refused to belong to either party...." (WA 60). In a time when "[e]verything was politics" and the fate of the whole nation seemed to depend on him, Christ told people that "he had nothing to do with politics, that his kingdom was not of this world." This was like saying "seek first God's kingdom" to a starving person (WA 62). Kierkegaard must have had this in mind when, in his earlier published "Open Letter" to Dr. Rudelbach, he emphasized that he had never called for disestablishment of the church, civil marriage, or "a single proposal for external change" (COR 53).

Yet in fact, political neutrality is actually an erroneous description of the scriptural point: Christ's mission *transcends* politics, challenging "the whole race" (i.e. all human persons) equally (WA 63-64). The call to faith and the love-commandments can never be reduced to any party stance; it is not on the same level as a voter who remains neutral on a major referendum. And seeking the eternal highest good "first" is entirely compatible with seeking to feed the starving person or correct structural injustices in the economic system "second"—not in temporal order but *within the conditions* involved in the first commitment. In other words, we can and should pursue finite earthly goods within the requirements of neighbor-love, including a merciful spirit, humility, and constant awareness that no combination of these goods amounts to the infinite good of salvation. For example, human beings are commanded to work "for the daily bread" of material necessities, which we do not get spontaneously like the bird or lily; but we should never "slave" for riches, which amounts to worshipping economic and social status, treating *comparative* material advantage as the highest (CD, "The Care of Poverty," 21).[14] Any

[14] Compare the journal entry in which Kierkegaard writes that "I have nothing against a person working for a living and the like" as long

"criterion of human comparison" is always fraudulent when it replaces our individual relation with God (WA, "Three Discourses at Communion on Fridays," 129).

Kierkegaard is rightly worried that "earthly and worldly care" for our future prospects can overshadow everything even when they are not focused on comparative differences; this amounts to avarice or "covetousness," a self-tormenting concern for economic advancement, displacing our devotion to God (CD 71-73). Similarly, conflating Christian faith with the actions of "general assemblies, synods, [or] balloting" is "profanization," encouraging people to measure their faithfulness by "comparison" with a circle of largely anonymous peers. But it does not follow that we can never take legitimate action via a general assembly or other political process (PV 134); people can pursue finite goods for their simple goodness rather than out of the corrupting motives of envy, concern for comparative place, or anxiety for social recognition. One can still earnestly love her family member even while her ultimate devotion to God requires her to side with God's word when family members reject these teachings (CD 183-4). Everything else is dethroned, subordinated to the ultimate love of God and duty to God. But she can remain involved with what is dethroned.

In sum, the justice thesis is compatible with the inwardness thesis: total outward withdrawal from pursuit of finite goods is not required. Kierkegaard recognized this in less rhetorically extreme moments, such as the passage in the "Open Letter" saying that while "Christianity is inwardness, inward deepening," if "the forms of life under which one has to live" are imperfect and can be improved, then "in God's name do so" (CA 53). Politics can be

---

as they don't presume to rationalize that their career success is necessary to witness to religious truth (PV 211, *Papier* X^2 A 98 *n.d.* 1849).

legitimate as long as it does not pretend to be the highest, or bastardize faith. Sometimes Kierkegaard's personal hatred of egalitarian movements in his own time got the better of him, prevented him from seeing that they might contain anything but the worship of Mammon instead of God. But my reconstruction seeks to purify what is defensible and insightful in his account from exaggerations that followed only from his personal blind spots, or pessimistic failings of sympathetic imagination.

In sum, according to this defensible reconstruction, we may legitimately care about, and strive for, finite earthly goods, including those elements of justice and social improvements that are the goals of worthwhile political movements, as long as these devotions are gathered together in our wholehearted commitment to the God who demands our unqualified love of all persons as neighbors, which overrides all other projects or cares when they contingently conflict. For example, that higher obligation could even require giving up our political or public career if the latter required violation of God's commands: devotion to our ultimate end saves us from merely consequentialist attitudes in promoting other worthwhile goods that social ethics may point out.[15] Thus, as Sylvia Walsh argues, in the *Postscript*, "natural human" appetites incline us towards aestheticism, but they can be worked on through our "universal-human" capacity for ethical willing, and both are preserved in a form purified of selfishness in the relation of faith in Christ.[16]

---

[15] See my essay, "The Ethical and Religious Significance of Taciturnus's Letter in Kierkegaard's *Stages on Life's Way*," in the *International Kierkegaard Commentary 11: Stages on Life's Way*, ed. Robert Perkins (Macon, GA: Mercer University Press, November 2000): 213-44.

[16] Sylvia Walsh, *Living Christianly* (Penn State University Press, 2005) 89-90.

III. Kierkegaard's Prescient Critiques of Political Religiousness and Populism

The defensible Christian attitude towards politics and social life constructed in the prior section still contains more radical implications than it may first appear. As Bob Perkins correctly stressed, the works we have considered anticipate Kierkegaard's final attack on Christendom in wholly rejecting any association of national and religious identity, because nations are aesthetic and historical phenomena.[17] His critique emphasizes that even well-intentioned political causes or reform campaigns can easily devolve into mere trend-following light-mindedness.[18] Then their ethical intent gives way to egoistic interests in being perceived as current or cool, i.e. coordinating with others' attitudes in order to blend in. People caught up in such coordination dynamics can easily forget that their individual relation to God cannot be mediated by social relations with other human persons, and least of all by political relations and patriotic loyalty. If religious commitments are steered by political goals, faith is conflated with some kind of group solidarity—a perversion that obscures the central purpose of religion in our lives.

Thus, even according to the balanced reconstruction of Kierkegaard's position, politics contains an ineradicable danger of profaning the highest ideal for human life.[19] The appeal of this *profanity thesis* is clearly explained in Stephen Backhouse's persuasive

---

[17] Perkins, "The Politics of Existence," 178.

[18] See Kierkegaard's Introduction to his *Two Ages* on "the demand of the age."

[19] I rely on the profanity thesis to prove that I have not simply offered a "toned down" or even "Mynsterian" version of Christianity here. Several defenders of agapic ethical ideals take similar positions. For example, arguably Levinas regards all notions of social contract or political agreement as inherently Hobbesian or self-interested. Derrida famously

account of Kierkegaard's reasons for rejecting "Christian nationalism." This phenomenon includes both a sense that one's national culture provides an edifying religious culture and the idea that such a culture represents a culminating stage in a historical accumulation of spiritual riches that the good Christian now inherits.[20] As Backhouse shows, both through Climacus and directly, Kierkegaard totally rejects Martensen's emphasis on contemporary civilization as "the necessary ingredient for Christianity." He also mocks N. Frederik Grundtvig's certainty that salvation lies in apostolic authority of the Danish church which sustains the community of believers through baptism; for this occludes the decisive importance of the individual's free choice in the effort to accept God.[21] The core of the problem, Backhouse rightly says, is that these approaches to religion teach people that faith is about being part of a historical identity group—an identity grounded in an era, a cultural heritage, or a set of popular movements.[22] In short, faith becomes historicized and turned into populist solidarity, with all manner of revivalists—both well-intentioned and not—using the basic human drive for social affiliation as a lever to get them to profess a religious identity.

---

made true justice into a kind of 'transcendental' that subtends familiar conceptions of political justice, which he views as inherently calculative and violent.

[20] See Stephen Backhouse, *Kierkegaard's Critique of Christian Nationalism* (Oxford University Press, 2011), for example pp.126-7.

[21] Ibid, 131-37. I am not saying that Kierkegaard's critique of Grundtvig was correct (I am not sure it was entirely fair, but Grundtvig surely connected popular Christianity with respect for "Nordic" cultural heritages, while also trying to help the poorer segments of society).

[22] Ibid, 138-9. Kierkegaard strongly insists that Christianity is "the religion of freedom;" even "God cannot take away from a human being" the inherent freedom of spirit which enables her *voluntarily* to give up "everything" in the world to follow Christ (CD, "What Shall We Have?," 179).

The problem at this fundamental level is not the inevitable need for statecraft or political communities, but the great crime of *manipulating* people's instinctive desire for acceptance to get them to conform to church or party identity or (worst of all) both without any autonomous conviction. This is the true meaning of "Christendom" for Kierkegaard: the reduction of faith to aestheticism. Politics brings a danger of profanization because it can weaponize people's natural need to belong to groups, rather than helping them to form social bonds based on ethical choice regulated by faith. The most extreme and thus glaring cases of this today include brainwashing to convince people to act as terrorists allegedly for their faith, which attracts young people looking for admiration and status. But the seeds of the same perversion are evident wherever politics eclipses the individual-God relation.

Thus Kierkegaard's critiques of both populist forms of pietism and the smug cultural superiority of the bourgeois link his arguments in the *Postscript* and "The Present Age" essay. Backhouse's assessment is insightful in suggesting that even if Kierkegaard's political inclinations made him look like a conservative who longs for a pre-modern form of traditional life without ostentation, in fact Kierkegaard's argument is *neither* politically liberal nor conservative. Neutrality returns: Kierkegaard's most important points about politics are not in the spirit of Wendell Berry's communitarianism, let alone the elitism of which Adorno accuses him.[23] There is nothing elitist or reactionary in resisting political movements that dupe and manipulate the so-called "common person" by playing on her fears of public ridicule or inadequacy relative to the most sophisticated or influential new trends. Aestheticism is bad enough in the libertine who fancies himself a romantic while actually treating others like dirt; but it is highly destructive when it becomes a force to get people to jump

[23]Ibid, 143-48.

on political bandwagons out of fear of being left behind, or not fitting in with peers. Even an enthusiastic religious community is horribly distorted when it is driven by panicky conformism that members cloak in "bad faith" about their motives.

The different pieces of Kierkegaard's view thus cohere well together. We can trace them, in part, to his transformative experience with the *Corsair* newspaper. The Hongs' introduction to *The Corsair Affair* explains how Kierkegaard thought that this scandal sheet had become a vehicle for the ethically disengaged "Byronic esthete" P.L. Møller to show off his wit while toying with the high society people of Copenhagen. *The Corsair* thus misused comic and ironic effects to promote a cynical countercultural superiority rather than to defend "a consistent and well-grounded ethical view."[24] The problem with the *Corsair*, then, was not that it attacked aristocrats, but rather that it promoted aesthetic spiritlessness: it seduced people into caring more about cruel gossip than any ethical reasons for political reform. Whereas the revolutionary age had shown that serious ethical commitment could take the form of political action, with people risking individual stands, the new mass media of the present age had appealed to people's basest motives in order to get sales. Papers like the *Corsair* branded themselves as arbiters of what's cool—the worst misuse of humor possible. The paper's juvenile attacks on Kierkegaard's looks and clothing, in response to his dare, only proved him absolutely correct on this.

Perhaps this public humiliation, despite the damage he did to the *Corsair*'s standing in the process, helped drive Kierkegaard towards the more extreme pessimism found in his last writings,

---

[24] See the Introduction to *The Corsair Affair*, ed. Howard V. Hong and Edna H. Hong (Princeton Univ. Press, 1982) xi-xvii, quoting Kierkegaard's *Two Ages*, 74.

motivating remarks which imply that a Christian can only contribute to society through becoming a sacrificial lamb (the martyrdom thesis noted earlier).[25] But for us today, this historical context only clarifies that the core of Kierkegaard's critique of politics—and popular culture more broadly—has real merit, no matter how his confessed melancholia led him to interpret the Danish Lutheran church of his day. Its central point turns out *not* to be that the average person in modern society is a deplorable sheep relative to great religious sages, but rather that too many *leaders* (including leading media figures) who set cultural movements treat her as if she were an empty cipher, a mere vessel for their messaging, rather than as a real person who deserves respect and help in developing ethical character. In other words, they use her through *aestheticizing* her religious sense, as noted above. This is a crime against both God and the people so used. Notably this critique can be endorsed even if we entertain (although Kierkegaard personally did not) the civic republican hope that democratic politics could be conceived as a pursuit of collective wisdom in discerning noble goals for social life, rather than as Plato portrayed it—an attempt to manipulate and appease mass appetites. For example, Habermasians should surely join Kierkegaard in condemning manipulation of people's religious sentiments for political purposes.

[25]In fact, Kierkegaard usually rejected literal demands for martyrdom in the *outward* sense that we must leave any earthly pursuits and seek some way to die for Christianity (e.g. see CD, "What Shall We Have?" 187). Rather, although we may have to risk great external losses or even our bodily lives (CD, *Discourses at the Communion on Fridays*, 259), it depends on God's grace what outward events may require of us. Thus in *Armed Neutrality*, he affirms that faith may require him to expose himself to becoming a martyr, but not to "flaunt a willingness for it" (which invites others to murder) or be "eager for it" (PV 135).

IV. Aestheticized Politics and Aestheticized Religion in the United States Today

The surprising result is that Kierkegaard's critique of mass politics, once dismissed as antisocial misanthropy or apathy in the face of earthly miseries, contains great insights with damning application to our contemporary scene. Kierkegaard's account of the corruption of both religious communities and high culture by populist political movements via mass media is uncannily relevant today. Although Kierkegaard was writing in a quite a different cultural situation over 170 years ago, the dangers he pointed out have proven to be perennial, with both outward and inward stakes now raised exponentially higher by the tremendous reach and permeation of internet media and social networking apps everywhere in our lives. Kierkegaard's concerns now appear so prescient and applicable across many nations that it is frightening.

The criticisms that follow are directed at all political sides in this nation. While I do not profess Kierkegaard's "neutrality," I condemn extremist tendencies on both the right and the left that are seducing Americans into self-righteous illusions of superiority. Without a change to our education, media, and constitutional structures soon, we may spend down the shrinking funds of trust and goodwill that keep this nation together (just as Chinese and Russian dictators hope).

My focus here is not on the content of partisan convictions, such as widespread certainty among Republicans that Democrats are unpatriotic, that there is too much immigration, that government is too large relative to the total economy, that abortion should be outlawed, or that we should somehow maintain open trade without any of our manufacturing jobs going overseas, etc.

Although many of these views are irrational, and few Americans understand either the federal budget or the constitutional flaws behind many dysfunctions in our federal government, such issues can be debated on the merits by responsible thinkers genuinely concerned for the common good of their nation.

Kierkegaard's analysis directs us instead to consider *the way* that people espouse these beliefs, or pretend to, to make a partisan persona for themselves. Many Trump enthusiasts are not actually moved by substantive ideas, arguments, or ethical commitments on the issues just listed, but are instead mainly driven by a desire for solidarity against other groups whom they dislike. The worship of right-wing radio hosts and online conspiracy theorists, and crazy fan loyalty at mega-rallies, often makes it facially apparent that ultra-partisan Trump supporters just want to feel *part of something*, to feel aggrandized by the power of the movement, and thus feel righteous and strong for a change. It is embarrassing to witness people clinging to patently empty slogans about greatness and chants calling for hostility to foreigners; the desperate lack of confidence in their own culture, learning, and ability to lead productive lives is sadly apparent at large Trump crowd events—I speak here from first-hand experience.

Many of these more combative right-wing types also correctly discern, without quite being able to articulate their resentment, that people on the far left have been increasingly enjoying a feeling of camaraderie by demonizing anyone who does not immediately kowtow to their ever-escalating demands for political correctness. It apparently feels great to many underachievers to brand others as intolerant relative to demands that everyone must endorse ever-more outlandish claims about systematic biases and oppressions of all kinds; the 'more-woke-than-thou' feeling of emotional superiority is especially intoxicating to many young people. So, people on the right want to feel the self-righteousness too, and get some crass payback in the process. Their feigned efforts to give plausible reasons for Trump policies are, for these marionettes of the right, mere rationalizations for enjoying the feeling of confirmation from many others who share their hatreds—just as among groups on the extreme left.

Thus the prevalence of bald machismo displays among Trump worshippers—a raw sense of hormonal self-assertion through large rifles and trucks with absurdly enormous wheels and oversized flags, sporting any sign that might shock liberals. I'm not referring here to Wall Street Republicans who are willing to bankrupt the nation if necessary to secure tax cuts for the rich. The guys and gals from the heartland aim instead to mark out a new cultural identity that they can see as both tough and pious. Once a group starts to form around this pitiful simulacrum of the "kalon"—something to provide a *sense of nobility* that they can apparently find nowhere else today—it becomes the focal point for a shared identity. Their friends and acquaintances have to get into this phenomenon, endorsing its creeds, if they want to be accepted: they must pledge allegiance to this zeitgeist, paraded with hats, smack talk about foreign groups and nations which they know little about, enthusiasm for gun shows and open carry, and posturing about military strength, all combined (disjointedly) with reassures that this is all about keeping (a)'merica "a Christian nation."

It's manifestly the belonging, not the issues, that are in the driver's seat for these people. Even among the small minority of Trump supporters brandishing one or another arcane racist symbol or going on about white identity being important "too," most probably have no truly autonomous racist commitments, reflected upon and actively affirmed. They are too *aesthetic* for that kind of real evil; they play at being racist, with one eye always nervously watching to make sure their peers are impressed. After all, Kanye West counts as a member of their gang as well. Many of them who imagine that they hate Muslims have never met one, and would probably have a great time with a Muslim guy who enjoyed competing with them in some test of nerves, before realizing that he was Muslim. Aestheticism here is not Kierkegaard's polite salon phenomenon, but it involves the same lack of earnest response to any deeply appreciated moral consideration. Political camaraderie, which allows each one to hide in the flag-waving mass, substitutes for frank honesty with oneself about both ethical standards and one's own ultimate commitments.

On the left, similar points apply to liberals who pretend interest in many social causes. Our sophisticate cultivates an online identity by liking a "Get Kony" page on Facebook, posting a couple of heartfelt comments about other social issues, and reviewing a recent action film (with a heartfelt note that its cast lacks 'body-type' diversity), before turning to the latest gossip about Kim Kardashian or some other celebrity. A minute is spent 'liking' a friend's post about children dying in Yemen (without any effort to understand the civil war there), and then its back to Kim. These things are all on the same plane to this master of whatever is trending; his apparent convictions are mere fashion statements to impress peers or (worse) himself with his sensitivity. When groups of people encourage each other to define themselves in this way, the vocabulary of the ethical is reduced to an emoji: they wear their momentary political causes like costumes for the week.

But there are also more extreme or fanatical social movements on the far left that believe they have a moral basis, such as those pushing the highly divisive and offensive language of "white supremacy," demanding that we all do endless penances and attain sensitivity trainings rather than seeking productive ways to improve concrete conditions for poor neighborhoods. We are also beset with insistences that there is no legitimate room for varying personal convictions on such deeply contested issues as gender identity and sexual mores; everyone must instantly accept any new conception of gender identities that a few have proclaimed as binding on us all.

Again, my claim is not that they are wrong on the issues; as it happens, I support gay marriage. Rather, the point is that self-righteousness and intolerance masquerade as earnestness in such movements, and the resulting high pressures to conform produce massive levels of false consciousness: many others parrot the new ways of speaking enforced by the cultural avant-garde, and try to make themselves believe they agree, when they are really just desperate to fit in, panicked about being branded an outcast if they do not speak "correctly" enough. Thus large masses are tyrannized by a few who use the coordination games of language and etiquette to enforce new norms on which they could never get reflective consensus in authentic rational argument. This desperate crowd-following makes serious discussion of ethically important identity issues impossible; a new Orwellian aura hangs over such topics. Even on the relative importance of these issues, dissent is construed as "disrespect" to make the unwary fall into line.

This is a new kind of "biopolitics" that the elites who use Foucaultian lingo to push the cultural envelope do not, interestingly, like to highlight. It produces psychic distortions by denying people the freedom to assess the relative importance of different social issues. Thus when the winter Olympics were held in Sochi, all the critics on western television were focused on oppression of gay people in Russia—which is certainly very bad, but hardly on a par with Putin helping Assad carry out genocide in Syria. Similarly, hate crimes against transgendered people are an anathema and deserve tougher sentences. But if social pressures make us think and speak as if transgender bathrooms are *as* morally urgent a social justice issue as lack of basic nutrition and medical care in the poorest nations, then group-think is out of control. In this environment a few popular figures who can influence the group-thinking will set the agenda for our attention.

Again, the point is not about the *content* of these political positions but about the way they are lived, enacted, and made into a basis for group identities, passcodes for acceptance. This is what Kierkegaard feared in reform movements of his own time—not that egalitarian proposals were wrong, but that pledging allegiance to them substituted for authentic individual commitment to any ideal, and handed over individual autonomy to the memes of the anonymous crowd. He saw this same problem in "awakenings" of mass religious fervor, especially when combined with poisonous nationalist rhetoric.

Which brings us to right-wing evangelical politics in America—the worst of all contemporary profanizations in Kierkegaard's sense. For decades now in the US, we have increasingly seen proclaimed religious affiliation itself used as another flag to add to the human peacock display, another sign to assure the others of one's solidarity with them (no matter what the issue or the statement). Think of the painfully feigned piety of the mass public prayer at large events, followed immediately by the national anthem or tributes to veterans so puffed with rhetorically exaggerated proofs of sincerity that their purely instrumental nature oozes from every word. Think of politicians dutifully appearing at the "Prayer Breakfasts" in DC to do homage to the clerics who now hold their dog chains.

This appalling spectacle is what religious faith has become to so many Americans. A thousand Pharisees and moneychangers could not in a year desecrate the Temple of faith so completely as one visit by our Vice President, who is apparently willing to brainwash his followers' minds for political ends, while he projects around himself a sanctimonious halo of piety so obviously artificial that only people under a kind of mind-spell could fall for it. Pretend faith is required for this *part* of the evangelical vote—for *of course* I do not say that all Americans who belong to evangelical churches are like this! So even Donald Trump now reads with mock-solemnity from the Bible in public to make us forget the way he used to rate women's body parts from 1-10 on the Howard Stern TV show. He is joined by Saint Newt Gingrich for whom Ayn Rand was Jesus's favorite disciple. Kierkegaard would have died of nausea if he had witnessed Americans being fooled by such shallow spectacles.

Again, this is not a criticism of evangelical churches or practices as such; nothing I say here is incompatible with evangelical spirit and emphasis on communal fellowship. Rather, I indict *the leaders* of some evangelical groups who have let their communities be so cynically used for political purposes—teaching their followers, for example, that supporting the Likud party's take-no-prisoners and grab-it-all strategies in Israel is synonymous with "supporting Israel" as such. This propaganda implies that anyone who criticizes the Likud or their ultra right allies must be an anti-Semite and want Israel destroyed. This is psychological trickery of the most cynical kind; for of course, one can oppose the Likud and want a peaceful two-state solution while still supporting Israel's right to exist (precisely as do many Israelis). To keep American voters in line, this propaganda pushes a false dichotomy and thereby denigrates all past victims of anti-Semitism. All this deception has been shamelessly undertaken to build a stronger voting coalition between economic libertarians, American Jews who understandably fear threats to Israel, and evangelicals who are taught that God wants all West Bank lands taken from the Arabs.

These and many similar mass consciousness phenomena in American politics have taken a huge toll on the nation. The rot of inauthenticity goes deep when some leaders on the right, including certain prominent Protestant and Catholic figures, are willing to fan conspiracy theories to get the Supreme Court picks they want. It apparently does not bother them that they are effectively in bed with Russian organized crime and kleptocracy as a result. These religious leaders in America are on a par with some leaders of the Russian Orthodox church who yoke their communities to Putin's fascist nationalism and thus support his mass murder in Syria and mockery of all international law in Crimea. These are *extreme profanizations*, fundamental violations of the duties of religious leaders. When surveying such deep betrayals, Kierkegaard's outrage at established churches become more comprehensible. At least in the cases I have cited, it would have been fully appropriate, and then some.

Kierkegaard's error was to focus too little on the leaders who shape trends in mass culture. He compared Goldschmidt, the editor of the *Corsair*, to a cholera fly who just happened to be the vessel through which the epidemic of false consciousness spread. In the United States, for over two decades now, Fox News has played the role of a *Corsair*, but of a far more lethal kind with exponentially greater effects. Here I will not fabricate any false equivalences: despite the narrow coverage now on MSNBC and CNN, they are not regime-controlled propaganda machines on a par with Fox News. Unlike the *Corsair*, Fox and the Murdoch family that owns it are not simply swept along by larger cultural forces; they are not mere cholera flies. Hannity, Ingram, Carlson and their backers have become main shapers of belief for almost half this nation. Their endless lies, distortions, hateful tirades, and conspiracy theories have so poisoned millions of minds that the populist movement they have inspired has become a social cancer, ostracizing anyone who does not pay homage to it in large parts of the US.

This was no accident: it was intentionally planned and executed by political and media leaders who *know very well* that they are systematically misrepresenting important realities: tax cuts do not pay for themselves; the caravan of refugees from Honduras was not filled with Middle Eastern terrorists organized by George Soros; coal does not employ more people than solar; there really are over a hundred deep connections between people in Trump's circle and Russian and Saudi bankers, fixers, and troll farm organizers; CNN is still fact-checked journalism. These Fox leaders are nothing like respectable conservative media organizations such as the *Wall Street Journal*; they are lying through their teeth. The tsunami of misinformation in which they have drowned this country is much like the Orwellian brainwashing portrayed in the movie *V for Vendetta*, with Hannity playing the bombastic "Voice of Britain" role. This is two orders of magnitude beyond anything Kierkegaard imagined and far more insidious. The joint operations of Fox and Russian social media manipulators are quickly rising to the level of Joseph Goebbels' masterful operations in the 1930s—not in content, but in methods.

Thus Kierkegaard is proven correct in the most awful way by the contemporary situation in the US. Politics done this way can corrupt literally every kind of activity and human practice that naturally has an ethical or religious telos. Mass manipulation of consciousness is a tool so powerful that it can overwhelm everything else. People's professed viewpoints on issues with serious impacts then become masks hiding confusion and fear of rejection underneath.

But politics does not need to be *this* profane. Kierkegaard did not try to articulate the possible political solutions to such redirections of religious faith into nationalist fervor, or reductions of communal solidarity into aesthetic group-think, exploiting people's desire for acceptance by others. The solutions include education: two nationally required courses, including one semester on basic civics, and another on logic and fallacies, would inoculate high school graduates from much misinformation. Massive campaigns against online propaganda and foreign hacking have also become necessary: we need to create very weighty deterrents against efforts by dictatorships to hijack our democratic discourse. Media reform is also vital: mass media will never be responsible when it is run mainly on the profit motive, as the rise of social media platforms like Facebook has proven once again. But even with such reforms, ethical leaders would remain crucial: we cannot salvage anything with leaders who are willing to poison their people's minds en mass. In particular, religious leaders must refuse and thwart anyone who would turn their faith into a political machine. If it requires martyrdom to prevent their faith from being co-opted by corrupt politicians, then martyrdom becomes part of their vocation after all.

Kierkegaard's Apocryphal Politics

M.G. Piety

There has been much discussion among scholars concerning the nature of Kierkegaard's political views.[1] Opinions on the substance of those views are widely diverging, however, and this is undoubtedly because Kierkegaard does not write in the straightforward style that has come to be typical of philosophers, at least since the period of the Enlightenment. His style has a certain affinity, as I have argued elsewhere,[2] with that of Plato in that he often expresses his views indirectly, through a variety of literary devices that include not only pseudonymity, but also hyperbole, irony, and humor. Kierkegaard's views, like those of Plato, are thus to a certain extent hidden beneath the surface of his writings. Hence the

[1] See, for example, *Kierkegaard: The Self In Society,* eds. George Pattison and Steven Shakespeare (Macmillan, 1998); *Foundations of Kierkegaard's Vision of Community,* eds. George Connell and C. Stephen Evans (Humanities Press, 1992); and Stephen Backhouse, *Kierkegaard's Critique of Christian Nationalism* (Oxford University Press, 2011). Backhouse's bibliography also lists numerous individual articles on the topic of Kierkegaard's political views that were not included in either the Pattison-Shakespeare or the Connell-Evans volumes.

[2] See "The Dangers of Indirection: Plato, Kierkegaard and Leo Strauss," in *Ethics, Love and Faith in Kierkegaard: Philosophical Engagements.* Ed. Edward Mooney (Indiana University Press, 2008), 163-74.

title of this talk. The term "apocryphal" comes from the Greek ἀπόκρυφος which means "hidden," or "concealed."[3]

"Kierkegaard's politics" is an inherently equivocal concept. It can be interpreted to mean either his expressly-held political views, or the political views that can reasonably be inferred from, or made to cohere with, his more general philosophical and theological views. Often, these two senses are conflated. It is important, however, to distinguish them. My project here is to examine in outline Kierkegaard's expressly-held political views, as well as what would appear to be the reasons and sentiment behind those views.

I

Kierkegaard's expressly-held political views are relatively easy to identify. The political implications of his thought, on the other hand, are more difficult to trace. Robert Perkins was among the first Kierkegaard scholars to point out how fundamentally social are the implications of Kierkegaard's thought. And there is now a growing body of scholarly literature devoted to showing that.[4] This project should in itself make clear, however, that Kierkegaard was not essentially a political thinker, at least not in the traditional sense, even if Perkins is correct, and I believe he is, in his view that Kierkegaard's thought has important positive social implications.

Kierkegaard is a religious thinker, of course, yet he inherited his religious views from Pietism and there is little evidence that he viewed himself as making an original contribution to the field of theology, at least not beyond the sense in which his psychological insights could be viewed as making such a contribution. Kierkegaard's primary interest is in the psychology of the individual,

---

[3] See *Greek-English Lexicon,* eds. Liddell, Scott, Jones (Oxford: Clarendon Press, 1968), http://stephanus.tlg.uci.edu/lsj/about.php.

[4] See note 1 above.

which is to say that his theoretical orientation is that of a psychologist. All traditional philosophical questions, not merely those concerning religion and ethics, but also those concerning epistemology and metaphysics are important, for Kierkegaard, only in terms of their significance relative to the individual as such.

This may be part of the reason that, as Stephen Backhouse observes in his book *Kierkegaard's Critique of Christian Nationalism*, Kierkegaard has often been viewed as a "radical, anti-social individualist."[5] This view is held by such important figures in the history of thought as Martin Buber, Karl Barth, Richard Niebuhr, Herbert Marcuse and Theodor Adorno.[6] Despite repeated efforts of contemporary scholars to retire this caricature of Kierkegaard[7] it continues to hold sway in the larger intellectual community as was witnessed by Peter Gordon's review of Daphne Hampson's *Kierkegaard: Exposition and Critique*[8] in *The New York Review of Books.*[9] Gordon describes Kierkegaard there as "an unbending conservative" whose "hatred of the mob...fosters...a disabling contempt for the public good."

Most contemporary Kierkegaard scholars realize, however, that Kierkegaard's expressed political conservatism did not stem from any sort of social elitism. He tended to identify, in fact, with

---

[5] Backhouse, 163.

[6] Ibid, "Kierkegaard and Society: The anti-social Kierkegaard?" 163-166.

[7] See, for example, ibid, "The social Kierkegaard" 166-169. This section of Backhouse's book contains a wealth of references to this attempt, including George Pattison and Stephen Shakespeare's *Kierkegaard: the Self and Society*, and George Connell and C. Stephen Evans, *Foundations of Kierkegaard's Vision of Community*.

[8] Daphne Hampson, *Kierkegaard: Exposition and Critique* (Oxford University Press, 2013).

[9] Peter Gordon, "Kierkegaard's Rebellion," *The New York Review of Books,* Nov. 10, 2016.

the common people,[10] which is not surprising considering this is the soil from which his father had sprung. Kierkegaard's conservatism is not an expression of contempt for the public good, but more an expression of his contempt for the mob, or more precisely, his cynicism concerning the ability of large groups of people to govern themselves humanely.

II

Kierkegaard was a monarchist. "Government [by] royal power is representative," he writes in a journal entry from 1847, "and to this extent Christian (monarchy)[.] The dialectic of monarchy is world-historically both well-established and unchanging" (KJN 4: NB 2.3). This is likely an allusion to Romans 13:1-7 where Paul asserts that "[e]veryone must submit to governing authorities. For all authority comes from God and those in positions of authority have been placed there by God."[11] That is, a monarch represents God, however imperfectly, in his or her role of governing a people, as well as representing the people themselves, to the extent that they also have a say in whether the monarch will remain in power and how extensive his or her powers will be.[12] The qualification "however imperfectly" is important because there is no reason to suppose Kierkegaard thought every monarch was equally good any more than there is reason to suppose that Paul thought all "governing authorities" were equally good. The meaning of Romans

[10] See, for example, Jørgen Bukdahl's *Søren Kierkegaard and the Common Man,* trans. Bruce H. Kirmmse (William B. Eerdmans Publishing, 2001).

[11] New Living Translation.

[12] See, for example, *The Concept of Anxiety,* trans. Reidar Thomte (Princeton University Press, 1980) 151 note.

13:1-7 is more likely, as David Papinaeu has argued,[13] that any government is better than no government in that it is a force for order, order without which human flourishing is impossible.

Kierkegaard was a monarchist,[14] not because he thought monarchs were invariably good, but because he had more faith in the individual than in any collective. Kierkegaard had reason, as I have argued elsewhere,[15] to be sanguine about the institution of monarchy. Frederik VI was a benign monarch. He instituted numerous progressive reforms, including freeing the serfs in 1788. Since Kierkegaard's own father, Michael Pedersen Kierkegaard, had been a serf, had it not been for the progressive views of Frederik VI, Kierkegaard would likely have been a serf as well and begun and ended his days on the same desolate Jutland heath where his father had herded sheep as a boy.

Frederik VI ruled Denmark for the first 26 years of Kierkegaard's life. Given that Kierkegaard lived to be only 42, that means Frederik VI ruled Denmark for most of Kierkegaard's life. Unfortunately, Frederik became more conservative after the French defeat in the Napoleonic Wars in 1814 and the loss of Norway by Denmark. Still, the Danish society in which Kierkegaard grew up

---

[13] "Even a bad state," observes Papineau, "is much better than none at all. When the hated regimes of Eastern Europe and South Africa collapsed at the end of the last century, their populations had the good sense to carry on recognizing the existing police, courts, and other state institutions until new constitutional arrangements could be made. By contrast, the misguided disbanding of the defeated Iraqi army and police by the US authorities in 2003 created a vacuum for mob rule, and is viewed by many commentators as the main source of the subsequent chaos in the Middle East. David Papineau, *Knowing the Score* (Basic Books, 2017), 58.

[14] See, for example, KJN 8: NB 23.

[15] See "Kierkegaard's Conservatism," *Piety on Kierkegaard,* January 22, 2017 https://pietyonkierkegaard.com/2017/01/22/kierkegaards-conservatism/.

was a product of his earlier progressive reforms.

A monarch, as an individual, and in particular as an individual standing alone, can be guided in his decision making by his conscience, or as Kierkegaard expresses it in the *Postscript,* by "the ethical only in himself," which, according to Kierkegaard, is his co-knowledge with God (CUP, 155; see also KJN 10: NB 36: 21), and which will hence be reliable even if his God-relationship is not what it ought to be. The same dynamic is more problematic, however, when a group rather than an individual holds the reins of political power. The greater the number of people involved in decision making, the harder it is for the individual to hear the voice of his or her conscience. The voice of conscience can be drowned out by the clatter of the mob. Hence the greater the number of people involved in decision making, the greater probability that decisions will be influenced by concerns other than those of conscience.

The difficulty, according to Kierkegaard, with political theorizing in the traditional sense is that it starts from a mistaken assumption. That is, it starts from the assumption that people are immanently capable of determining a just order of society, as well as of implementing and sustaining this order. But this assumption rests in turn on another assumption that Kierkegaard categorically rejects: that people are fundamentally good-willed toward one another. It's not that Kierkegaard has such a negative view of human nature that he thinks people are unrelentingly ill-willed toward one another. The problem, for Kierkegaard, is that the human will is divided. It wants the flourishing of the neighbor, but it wants as well a flourishing for itself that it sees as at least occasionally opposed to the neighbor's flourishing. Or to put the problem in more theological terms: the will wants to conform itself to God's will, yet also wants to be self determining.

Only by relating ourselves properly to God is it possible, according to Kierkegaard, for us to understand how to relate properly to our neighbor. "[L]ove for God," he explains, "is the decisive factor; from this originates love for the neighbor.... [I]n love for the neighbor," Kierkegaard continues,

> God is the middle term. Love God above all else; then you also love the neighbor and in the neighbor every human being. Only by loving God above all else can one love the neighbor in the other human being. The other human being, this is the neighbor who is the other human being in the sense that the other human being is every other human being (WL, 57-58).

Nowhere is this made clearer than in chapter VII of the second part of *Works of Love.* The chapter begins with the biblical injunction "Do not forget to do good and to share" [Heb 13:16]—but do not forget either," warns Kierkegaard,

> that this incessant talk by worldliness about beneficence and benevolence and generosity and charitable donations and gift upon gift is almost merciless. Ah, let the newspaper writers and tax collectors and the parish beadles talk about generosity and count and count; but let us never ignore that Christianity speaks essentially of mercifulness, that *Christianity would least of all be guilty of mercilessness*....But people prattle and prate ecclesiastically-worldly and worldly-ecclesiastically about generosity, beneficence—but forget, even in the sermon, mercifulness. From the Christian point of view, this is an impropriety.... *Woe to him who devours the inheritance of widows and the fatherless* [Matt. 23:14], but woe also to the preacher who is silent about mercifulness in order to talk about generosity! Preaching should indeed be solely and only about mercifulness. If you know how to speak effectually [*tilgavns*] *about this*, then generosity [*Gavmildhed*] *will follow of itself* and *come by itself* accordingly as the individual is capable of

it (WL, 315, emphasis added).

It is clear from this passage from *Works of Love,* a work published under Kierkegaard's own name rather than a pseudonym, that Kierkegaard believes we have a duty to do good and to share. That is, it is clear he believes we have a duty to help one another in a practical sense, to ameliorate the deficiencies in others' material circumstances. It is equally clear, however, that he traces those deficiencies to a spiritual poverty whose amelioration is more urgent in that once it is taken care of, material generosity "will follow of itself."

III

As I mentioned at the beginning of this essay, one of the difficulties scholars face in attempting to understand Kierkegaard is that Kierkegaard does not present his views in the straightforward way we have come to expect of philosophers. I also observed, however, that in this respect he is in good company. Plato, arguably the greatest philosopher in the history of Western thought, if not in the history of thought more generally, declined to present his views directly, but forced his readers to delve beneath the surface of his works in an effort to divine their meaning. The German classicist Norbert Blössner argues in a wonderful essay entitled "The City-Soul Analogy,"[16] that contrary to what generations of Plato scholars have thought, the *Republic* is not primarily a piece of political philosophy but a piece of moral philosophy. The entire city-soul analogy, he argues, is a rhetorical device employed by Plato in the service of the argument that it is better to be just than unjust.

[16] Norbert Blössner, "The City-Soul Analogy," in *The Cambridge Companion to Plato's Republic,* ed. G.R.F. Ferrari (Cambridge University Press, 2007) 345-385.

Knowledge of the Good is prerequisite, argues Socrates in the *Republic,* to genuine knowledge of what is just.[17] The difficulty, of course, is that most people, according to Socrates, lack knowledge of the Good, and hence of justice. Not only are most people ignorant of the Good, they are, in fact, not even oriented properly relative to it. That is, they are not "approaching it as a proselyte," to use a phrase from Kierkegaard's *Philosophical Crumbs,*[18] but are facing *away* from it.[19] They must be turned around, or "converted to the light from the darkness" (στρέφειν πρὸς τὸ φανὸν ἐξ τοῦ σκοτώδους).[20]

Only once such a "conversion" has taken place in the individual, asserts Socrates, can he attain the proper relation to the Good and hence genuine knowledge of justice. And only once such knowledge is attained, can there be any talk of constructing a just city.

And yet, observes Blössner, "it is important for Socrates' argument that the city shapes the souls of its citizens and their conceptions of happiness and that it creates the framework within which those conceptions are either easier or more difficult to realize."[21] That is, the *Republic* is, in a sense, a political work, even if its ultimate objective is the conversion of the individual from darkness to light.

---

[17]. See *Republic* 506a-b.

[18] Søren Kierkegaard, *Repetition and Philosophical Crumbs*, trans. M.G. Piety (New York: Oxford University Press, 2009), 92.

[19] Ibid, 91.

[20] *Plato VI Republic Books 6-10,* tran. Paul Shorey (*The Loeb Classical Library,* 1935) 518c5-7. The expression Plato uses here for "converted" is στέφω, the same expression that is translated as "converted" in the King James rendering of Matt 18:3.

[21] Blössner, 383.

The same thing can be said of Kierkegaard's works. His primary concern is always the spiritual situation of the *individual*, or the conversion of the individual from the darkness of what he believed was the bourgeois pseudo-Christianity that dominated the Denmark of his day to the light of authentic Christianity. And yet, he conceived of himself as the spiritual watchman of his own city.[22] "I love my native land," he wrote in his journal in 1848, "it is true that I have not gone to war— but I believe I have served it in another way…." (PV, 170/JP 6: 6259).[23]

Kierkegaard wrote in Danish for fellow Danes whom he felt had lost their spiritual way. So although his primary concern, like Plato's, is with the individual, it is clear that, again like Plato, he understood the intimate connection between the city and humankind and hence the political implications of his thought.

"[I]f what one sees all over Europe is Christendom," Kierkegaard wrote in his journal in 1849, "then I propose to start here in Denmark to list the price for being Christian in such a way that the whole concept—state church, official appointments, livelihood—bursts open" (PV, 201/JP 6:6444).

Kierkegaard's Denmark, or perhaps for the purposes of alliteration I may be allowed to say Kierkegaard's Copenhagen, shaped the souls of its citizens just as Plato's Athens shaped the souls of *its* citizen. Kierkegaard's Copenhagen shaped its citizens' concep-

---

[22] The pseudonym under which *The Concept of Anxiety* appeared was Vigilius Haufniensis which translated literally as "watchman of Copenhagen."

[23] It is interesting to note here that while Kierkegaard may not have been nationalistic, at least in the sense of Christian nationalism, he was patriotic in the sense in which Robert Audi discusses what he argues is the difference between nationalism and patriotism. See Audi, "Nationalism, Patriotism, and Cosmopolitanism in an Age of Globalization," *The Journal of Ethics,* 13, 2009, 365-381.

tions of Christianity and created a framework within which, according to Kierkegaard, a proper understanding of Christianity was difficult to attain.

Thus Kierkegaard, like Plato, set for himself the task of helping his compatriots, one individual at a time.

Kierkegaard on Politics: Putting the Modern State in its Place While Loving Our Neighbors

C. Stephen Evans

This essay is written in honor of Robert Perkins, and I want to begin by expressing my gratitude for his life and work. Robert Perkins nurtured several generations of Kierkegaard scholars, and a great many of us would not have accomplished whatever we have accomplished without his help and encouragement.

From the time I first knew Bob he told me that he wanted to develop an extended account of Kierkegaard's political theory. To the best of my knowledge the book-length version of this work never appeared, though Bob certainly made contributions in this area.[1] The reasons are no doubt various. It certainly was not because Bob Perkins did not work hard. Anyone who tries to read through the *International Kierkegaard Commentary* series will be in awe of the prodigious work the project involved. Perhaps one reason the book-length work in political theory did not appear was

---

[1] See, for example, Robert Perkins, "The Politics of Existence: Buber and Kierkegaard," in *Kierkegaard in Post/Modernity*, ed. Martin Matuštik and Merold Westphal (Indiana Univ. Press, 1995) 167-81.

because Bob was so unselfish. He gave so much of his time to helping others that it was not possible for him to do everything he himself had wanted to do. However, I think another reason is that the materials in the Kierkegaard corpus are too skimpy really to allow for the development of an account of anything that deserves to be called "Kierkegaard's political theory."

This lack of materials is no accident. Kierkegaard does not really provide a political theory because he was not deeply interested in politics, and there is a substantive reason for this relative lack of interest. There is a huge divide that permeates the whole of Kierkegaard's authorship. That divide is described in different language at different times, but it is fundamentally the distinction between what is absolute and what is relative, what is eternal and what is temporal, what is absolutely essential and what is contingent. The political sphere falls clearly within the domain of the relative, the temporal, and the contingent. As Johannes Climacus says in *Concluding Unscientific Postscript,* the human task is to seek to achieve an absolute relation to the absolute and a relative relation to the relative. I know of no writer who focused more on what is absolute and essential than Kierkegaard did. His attention was always directed at the absolute, and his gaze was both intense and unrelenting.

Of course this does not mean that what is relative, including politics, has no importance at all, and Kierkegaard does have things to say about politics. Later in this paper I will discuss the political implications of one of his most significant concepts. However, it is important first to focus on the limits of the political. What does it mean to say that something has only relative importance? How shall we draw the distinction between what is absolute and what is relative? I think for Kierkegaard the distinction amounts to this: What is absolute must be relevant to every human life, and it must be something that makes it possible for every human life to have intrinsic meaning and value. When measured by this criterion, the political cannot be absolute.

For example, Kierkegaard insists that the meaningfulness and value of a human life is not determined by its world-historical significance. A clear statement of this claim can be found in the extended argument that Johannes Climacus provides in *Concluding Unscientific Postscript* that world-historical significance is not part of what we might call the essential human task (CUP, 130-59). The argument is that to make the meaning of human life to depend on history is to embrace a despairing view of human life (CUP, 133). If, however, we understand the meaning of human life as achieving ethical character, then the life of a person who is unfortunate enough to live under a despotic tyrant can be just as meaningful as the life of a person who lives in a time of relative freedom and enlightenment. For all human persons live "before God." All are accountable to God. The task is to be faithful to one's calling, and whether one has a calling cannot depend on whether one is fortunate or unfortunate, privileged or destitute, politically influential or completely powerless. Whether one lives in a democracy, or must be obedient to an absolute monarch, or is oppressed by a dictator, cannot be decisive in the sense that the meaning and value of a person's life depends on such contingent factors.

Perhaps one thing then that we can learn from Kierkegaard is that politics is not all-important. Hegel famously claimed that the modern period was the end of history, and he claimed that the meaning of human life required an understanding of the course of history. We live at the end of history because we have seen the development of the modern liberal state, in which every person is equal and free. Such a state represents the overcoming of the opposition between the individual and community. Hence for Hegel the identity of the modern individual is found in the modern state, which is the expression of the freedom and rationality the individual seeks.

Kierkegaard disagrees fundamentally with such a view, and he wants to put the modern state in its place. He admits that it is possible that human history has an objective meaning, but he claims that if so it can only be discerned by God (CUP, 141). The meaning of an individual's life cannot depend on what period of history one happens to live in, or upon understanding the place of one's historical age in the grand story that God alone knows. Every individual has the task of becoming the self God wills the individual to become, and this is a task that can in principle be carried out in any time and in any political circumstance. The Hegelian view is seen by Kierkegaard as a kind of human collective self-deification, and Hegel's philosophy is the esoteric expression of the exoteric triumphalism of Christendom.

So politics is not all-important for Kierkegaard. The kind of political system one finds oneself in cannot be of ultimate importance, either, and the modern state provides an identity for individuals only by becoming an idol. I think an important lesson can be learned here. Kierkegaard himself said that "[i]n these times everything is politics," and he meant that as a criticism (PV, 103).

In the current period, especially in the United States, it is all too tempting to become obsessed with politics.[2] The media is dominated by a president who seems to have the gift of calling up every vile aspect of American character. Racism and nationalism have become increasingly prominent. Orwell's concept of the "Big Lie," which Orwell saw as the trademark of authoritarian governments of the left and the right, has become a daily affair. In such a situation it is easy to think that opposition to such a political

[2] This essay was written during the first presidential term of Donald Trump.

movement is of absolute importance. I think Kierkegaard would want to remind us that such opposition may be important, but it is not absolutely important. We should do whatever we can to oppose such evil, but we must not succumb to despair if our political efforts fail. Nor should we think that the kingdom of God is at hand if our political efforts succeed. It is healthy to be reminded that our lives, and the lives of our contemporaries, have meaning and value regardless of how bad or how good the political situation is.

Still, I believe there is something of value for politics in Kierkegaard's thought. The primary source of that value is his faith in human equality or *Menneske-Lighed.* Kierkegaard believed very deeply that in an important sense every human person has intrinsic worth and value, and that this value is equal in the sense that the value of a human life is incommensurable and cannot be made a matter of degree. In fact, this conviction serves as a kind of touchstone for how Kierkegaard looked at worldviews. To accept a philosophy or worldview that empties some human lives of meaning and worth is not only to accept a false view; it is to become a kind of traitor to the human race. We have an ethical duty to reject such ways of thinking.

This commitment to human equality can be seen in many facets of Kierkegaard's work. To take just one example that seems unrelated to ethical or political issues, in *Philosophical Fragments* Johannes Climacus affirms a principle of human equality in looking at the role historical evidence might play in coming to have a relationship to God. Making faith depend on evidence that is not universally available is repugnant to Climacus: "Would the god allow the power of time to decide whom he would grant his favor, or would it not be worthy of the god to make the reconciliation equally difficult for every human being at every time and in every place" (PF, 106).

This ideal of equality is grounded in the claim, deeply embedded in *Works of Love,* that every human being possesses an "inner glory," one that can only be seen in the light of eternity (WL, 88). Kierkegaard here compares human persons to sheets of fine stationery. Each sheet may have something different written on it, but when one holds the pieces up to the light, they all possess the same watermark. Similarly, human persons are all different, but when they are seen "by eternity's light," they all are similar and possess an inner glory (WL, 89). This is why Kierkegaard, though stressing the claim that our duty to love the neighbor is grounded in God's command, is not an ethical voluntarist. God's command to love the neighbor is in no way arbitrary, but is a command to recognize and respect the value God has placed in every person.

Kierkegaard understands that this ideal of equality is one that has political implications. He says that a politician looking at Kierkegaard's writings may think that there is nothing of value to be found. However, Kierkegaard claims that if this politician "would kindly be a little patient," he will perhaps recognize that Kierkegaard's religious vision is "the transfigured rendition of what a politician, provided he actually loves being a human being and loves humankind, has thought in his most blissful moment" (PV, 103).

To be sure, just after having articulated this ideal and hinting that it does have political significance, Kierkegaard seems to empty the idea of political relevance by claiming that "no politics is able...to think through or to actualize...this idea of human equality" (PV, 103). The basis for this claim is Kierkegaard's belief that it is simply not possible to achieve a society in which humans would be equal in such "worldly" aspects as wealth, power, and intelligence. In *Works of Love,* he argues that the person who loves the neighbor, rather than seeking to establish worldly equality through political action, should "rise above" all earthly dissimilarities and love all humans, regardless of their worldly status. "Christianity, then, does not want to take away the dissimilarity, neither of high rank nor of lowliness" (WL, 71).

Kierkegaard is right in thinking that perfect equality of status, wealth, power, and influence is an unrealizable, utopian ideal. No matter how just a human society may be, inequalities of various kinds will always be present. There will always be "dissimilarities" that constitute "temptations" that the person who loves the neighbor must rise above. However, even if he is right about this, it does not follow that the one who loves the neighbor will be indifferent about every form of inequality that is present or be willing to tolerate every kind of inequality.

Kierkegaard himself implicitly admits this when he recognizes the impact the idea of equality has had on modern societies. He believes this idea of equality has its source in Christianity and Judaism. Whatever the source, Kierkegaard clearly approves of the abolition of slavery and feudalism: "The times are past when only the powerful and the prominent were human beings—and the others were bond-servants or slaves. This is due to Christianity" (WL, 74). He makes similar remarks about changes in status for women: "What abominations has the world not seen in the relationships between man and woman, that she, almost like an animal, was a disdained being in comparison with the man, a being of another species" (WL, 138).

Now it must be admitted that Kierkegaard couples these remarks with a remarkable indifference or even hostility to contemporary proposals for social changes, including full emancipation for women. However, I think we ought to distinguish between the logical implications of Kierkegaard's ideas and his own personal political proclivities. He clearly recognizes that the principle of human equality is incompatible with slavery and at least some ways of treating women. I do not see any principled reason why he should not be willing to consider concrete proposals for further social and political changes that are motivated by the idea that every human being has dignity, an equal worth and value.

This is the case, even if Kierkegaard is right in thinking that perfect worldly equality is neither possible nor desirable. It may be true that schemes for advancing human equality may have unintended and unforeseen consequences, resulting in greater injustice and inequality rather than less. But it does not follow from this fact that political proposals to eliminate forms of injustice and forms of inequality are always useless or pointless. It may be true, as Jesus said, that we will always have people who are poor in our communities, at least in a relative sense. But it does not follow from this that it is acceptable for a society to concentrate nearly all its wealth and power in the top 1% of the population.

Surely, the idea of human equality that Kierkegaard accepts at least rules out forms of racism, nationalism, and sexism, which fail to recognize the full value and worth of some persons. It seems to me that proposals to advance equality and limit the "temptations" Kierkegaard admits we encounter from inequality must be evaluated on the basis of practical reason. It might be, for example, that state ownership of the means of production, which was thought by Marxists to advance economic equality, actually worsens inequality. But even if this is so, it does not mean that no economic policies or programs can be defended as grounded in the equal worth of humans. Think, for example, of government policies that treat healthcare as a basic right of all citizens, or even all residents of a country. Every developed country with the exception of the USA seems to have implemented such a policy, and surely some of the policies can be shown empirically to work well. Is this not a way of recognizing the equality of all human persons?

I conclude that although Kierkegaard certainly would never view any political outcome or movement as of ultimate importance, it does not follow that the individual who is seeking to become the self God intends the person to be will not be involved in political work. Furthermore, such political work should be shaped by such fundamental ethical truths as the basic equality humans enjoy as children of God. Such work may be more prominent in some callings than others; not everyone is called to enter politics or become a political organizer. However, in a democracy I believe all of us have some obligations to work towards a society that recognizes the value and work of every human being. We will not thereby bring about the kingdom of God, but we may very well make the lives of our neighbors somewhat better, and thereby show in a concrete way that our love is genuine.

Kierkegaard would, I think, rightly remind us of the limits of the political sphere. Our duties to love our neighbors cannot be exhausted simply by supporting the right political causes. We must always seek to love others in concrete ways in the particular circumstances of our daily lives. We have a duty to "love the people we see," and Kierkegaard thinks that means that we ought to love the people we rub shoulders with on a daily basis (WL, 154-74). Kierkegaard is rightly critical of the individual who loudly supports political change to benefit the masses, while holding himself aloof from actual contact with those of lower social and economic status. Kierkegaard himself went on daily walks in Copenhagen where he made it a point to converse with people of all social classes. Political action should not be a substitute for caring for concrete individuals in our daily lives, and it is farcical to "love humanity" but despise the person who lives next door. However, to say that politics is not everything is not to say it is nothing. Our political lives can attempt to embody a care for the good of others, even if the particular policies this care justifies may be the subject of reasonable debate.

Stepping Forward in Character—But Onto What Stage? Arendtian Reflections on Kierkegaardian Anti-politics

George Pattison

Introduction

Hannah Arendt's essay *The Human Condition* is driven by a deep worry that as 'politics' gets progressively taken over by economic management Western societies are losing their capacity for political action. But this is more than just a matter of social change. It also affects what it is to be human, since participation in genuine political life is, in Arendt's view (following Aristotle), both a condition and an expression of personality in its fullest sense. However, action is not to be confused with throwing a bomb, blocking a highway, or picketing a school. The primary form of action, according to Arendt, is speaking and, with direct reference to Aristotle, she claims that it is "speech" that "makes man a political being."[1] To step forward in an assembly of one's peers and to speak is, as we say, 'to make a statement', which is more than just saying

[1] Hannah Arendt, *The Human Condition* (Chicago: Chicago University Press, 1958) 3.

something. To make a statement is to stake out a position, to show a way forward, or to place an obstacle in the way of some contrary policy. In such contexts, our words define us and reveal what we stand for and how far we are prepared to go so that the action of those who step forward in this way defines the nature of the polis, the political community. As Arendt puts it, the political is "the space where I appear to others as others appear to me, where men exist not merely like other living or inanimate things but make their appearance explicitly."[2]

These remarks throw light on what it might mean to call Kierkegaard a "political" author—despite his own assertion that "politics is not for me" (LD, 184). In particular, they throw light on his constant preoccupation in the latter part of the 1840s with the future direction of his authorship, which, in turn, is connected to his endless ditherings over whether to publish his new work pseudonymously, under his own name, or even whether to publish it at all. Strikingly, Arendt's basic metaphor of stepping forward into public space so as to appear as who one is seems very precisely to capture what is at issue in these journal ponderings.

Urbanity, Citizenship, and the Political

We shall return to this metaphor shortly, but to see more of what is at issue here I should like first to explore three terms that have some overlap but are also significantly distinct: urbanity, citizenship, and politics. All of these terms relate to Latin or Greek words for 'city' but, in each case, mean something more than or slightly different from a simple numerical ensemble of buildings and populations. As we shall see, each also brings out a particular aspect of Kierkegaard's relation to his own city, Copenhagen. In a certain

[2] Ibid, 198-9.

sense, they can even be seen as relating to the three familiar categories of the aesthetic, the ethical, and the religious.

In the case of urbanity, the term is Latin, and relates in the first instance to one city, the eternal city, Rome. This is something different from the Greek city-state, since, in the course of its development, this particular city-state became the capital of a world-empire in which a multitude of cultures and traditions co-existed in complex ways, sometimes finding fruitful synergies and sometimes descending into communal violence. The history of the relationship between Rome and Christianity is itself illustrative of both possibilities. But whatever the exact state of play at any given moment, to be urbane is to be able to negotiate this complex social space with ease and assurance. This not only implies a fundamental distinction between the city-dweller, with his polished manners and refined habits, and the country-dweller, with his rough-hewn homespun ways. It also suggests a certain proximity to power, even if one is not oneself concerned with the exercise of power.

That Kierkegaard was "urbane" is perhaps the easiest and least controversial thing to say of him. Certainly he cultivated in a self-conscious way qualities that we might describe as urbane. Already in the Gilleleie Journal, Kierkegaard speaks of himself (or of the fictive character who, on a certain view, is the journal's subject) as "a man dressed in modern clothes, wearing spectacles, and smoking a cigar" and, as such, standing out from the North Sjælland country-folk amongst whom he is travelling (JP 5094/KJN 1: AA1, 4). The same self-consciousness of being a 'man of the city' emerges in the (much debated) journal of his trip to Jutland in 1840, where, writing from Aarhus on 18 July, he comments "Life in these market-towns is just as wretched, ridiculous and *abgeshmackt* [insipid] as the gait one adopts in the streets. In vain does one endeavour to appear with any dignity...—and if one also remembers that one is an object of curiosity so peculiar to market-towns', adding a brief note, "NB," on "The wolfish hunger of country-townsmen for 'news from the capital…" (here, however, he makes a distinction between such people and genuine country people, who have "an independent life"—he is, after all, on a pilgrimage to the place where the country people who were his own ancestors had their home) (JP 5452, 5453/ KJN 3, NB 6:2, 188, translation amended). The key point here is the self-consciousness of one who is urbane in the strong sense, a man from the capital.

What this means is explored in more depth—or, perhaps we should say, exhibited in all its superficiality—at many points in the authorship. To be sure, Kierkegaard's urbanity is most on display in various of the pseudonyms, in the Seducer, in Constantin Constantius, or in Johannes Climacus, but it also surfaces in writings appearing under his own name. Indeed, it is so pervasive that, even when the context is clearly fictional we cannot dissociate it from a construction of urbanity that plays a strategic role in the authorship. The theatre, cafés, exhibitions, parks, carriage-rides, train journeys, cigars, spectacles, and clothes all play their part in this construction. Perhaps the most renowned episode, the part that stands for the whole, is Johannes Climacus' meditation in Frederiksberg Gardens, sitting in Josty's café, smoking his cigar, and pondering the many ways in which the "many benefactors of the age" have been making life easier and easier, "some by means of railways, others with omnibuses and steamships, others with the telegraph, others with easy to read surveys and short summaries of everything worth knowing" (CUP, 185-8, translation amended). The passage is given added significance by being identified by its author as the moment in which he discovered his literary vocation—to make something more difficult.

The splicing of such moments of sheer urbanity with the genesis of the authorship is also hinted at, although in more ambiguous and complex ways, in *The Point of View*, where, although bearing witness that when *Either/Or* was written he was already, religiously speaking, in the monastery, Kierkegaard describes how he took pains—successfully—to create a quite opposite image of himself: "If Copenhagen has ever been of one opinion about anybody, I venture to say that it was of one opinion about me, that I was an idler (*Dagdriver*), a dawdler, a flâneur…I represented a worldly irony, joie de vivre, the most refined form of pleasure-seeking—without a trace of 'seriousness and positivity;' on the other hand, I was prodigiously interesting and piquant" (PV, 61/SKS 16: 42, translation amended). Strikingly, Kierkegaard here uses the French term "flâneur"—spicing his sentences with such other loan words from French as "*raffinerede*" and "*piquant.*" It almost goes without saying that, in the century in which Paris could claim to be the cultural capital of the world, French was also the language par excellence of urban sophistication.

In identifying himself as such a flâneur, Kierkegaard allies himself in advance to the archetypal image of the flâneur that would be developed shortly afterwards in the work of Baudelaire, the supremely urban poet, "a lyrical poet in the era of capitalism" as Benjamin would describe him.[3] Whether in Baudelaire or in Kierkegaard, this is, of course, a deeply conflicted role. But at least part of the pose in the Parisian variant, as in Kierkegaard's own case, is a conservative approach to modern political developments, and a negative attitude towards widening democracy as symptomatic of the impending triumph of the masses. The flâneur, urban man that he is, even, in a sense, as a man of the crowd, is also, always, a man who stands apart, who looks at the world through his lorgnette, critical, distanced, unengaged.

Whether Kierkegaard was entirely successful in carrying through his pose of being such a flâneur is open to question. Baudelaire, after all, had Paris, but Kierkegaard, for all his French loan

---

[3] See Walter Benjamin, *Charles Baudelaire: A Lyric Poet in the Era of High Capitalism*, trans. Harry Zohn (London: New Left Books, 1973).

words, had only Copenhagen and, even if Copenhagen was the capital of Denmark, it was, he often came to think, no better than Aarhus, a mere "market-town" consumed by a market-town curiosity about anyone who stood out from the ordinary. In striving to express urbanity, Kierkegaard was not only playing a self-conscious (and arguably deceptive) role, he was also having to work against rather than to express the social conditions of his existence—at least on his own, post-Corsair view of things.

We come to the second category, that of the citizen. Many Parisian flâneurs were also citizens. Kierkegaard too was a citizen. But if this suggests a range of rights and responsibilities, a place in the public sphere, it does not of itself immediately involve or require political activity, in the sense in which we understand the term. A citizen can own property, act as a legal person, become a member of the Church, study at university, enter into professional life, publish, petition the monarch, and many other things. In democracies, citizens also have a right to play their part in political life, but for much of Kierkegaard's life, that part was extremely limited. Even some of the rights of citizenship were limited—e.g., there were significant restrictions not only on Jews but also on Catholics.

How far did Kierkegaard understand himself as a citizen? The pseudonym Vigilius Haufniensis is suggestive: what could be a more appropriate role for one who understood the obligation incumbent on any good citizen to watch over the city and be guardian of its well-being. But how might Kierkegaard's authorship reflect such a self-appointed role? Here the encounter with *The Corsair* is, perhaps, paradigmatic. Kierkegaard himself refers to it in an article of January 1846 as "a literary police action" (COR, 47-50/SKS 14: 85-9). His role, as he seems to see it, is precisely to act on behalf of the stability and order of the city against an organ that is continually running up against the boundaries of civic decency, to protest, on behalf of civic order, against the "rabble-barbarism" that *The Corsair* represented. Interestingly, perhaps, although *The Corsair* did have a *political* angle, in the sense of promoting a Republican agenda, this is scarcely if at all touched on in Kierkegaard's polemics or even his journal articles dealing with *The Corsair*. The issue seems to be far more one of ensuring that private citizens are free to go about their legal business and that the language of the public sphere maintains a certain level of civility. In this respect, Kierkegaard's intervention in the affairs of *The Corsair* is at the sophisticated end of a kind of literature that involves societal comment, but of a non-political kind. The lower end was represented by the contemporary journal *Politievennen* ("The Policeman's Friend," perhaps) in which articles appeared drawing attention to various forms of bad behavior that needed correction—such as the woman who took the entrance money to the Round Tower but was regularly seen to be absent, disporting herself with young men.[4]

Assessor Vilhelm and the ethical point of view that he represents is probably the strongest voice on behalf of the claims of civic responsibility and life in the context of the authorship: Kierkegaard's pre-emptive defence, as it were, against the accusation that both the event of the broken engagement and the possibility of "the exception" were intended as a general criticism of the social order. Whatever else we make of the Assessor, he seems to be there to underline the point that Kierkegaard is writing throughout as a private, single individual, and not as the proponent of a social programme. The space of the exception is circumscribed in advance by acceptance of a world of families, work, and public responsibility. As Kierkegaard put it in conversation with King Christian VIII: "I regarded my entire work to be beneficial also to

[4] Another example of such a "police action" could be Kierkegaard's speech on the freedom of the press to the Student Association in 1835.

any government, but the point of it was that I was and would remain a private citizen" (JP 6309/KJN 5: NB9: 41, 228).

Like "urbanity" and "citizenship" the word "politics" relates back to the ancient world's experience of city life. Whether in ancient or modern times, however, it is clear that not everyone who inhabits the city (understood as a geographical entity) is party to its political life in exactly the same way. In ancient times it was accepted that, e.g., slaves or women were not citizens in the same way as free men and therefore not entitled to participate in decision-making affecting public life. In modern times, many city-dwellers, e.g., illegal immigrants, are not citizens in the same sense as others. Even human rights legislation that extends protection and rights to all, irrespective of citizenship narrowly defined, often serves only to mitigate, not to cancel the negative aspects of this situation. On the other hand, even those who possess the political rights of full citizens do not always use them. Throughout the developed world, citizenship is offered, in principle, as broadly as possible to all inhabitants of any given polity, yet declining numbers of people actually vote in elections and even fewer take an active part in political life.

In an era of democratic politics, the line between active citizenship and full participation in political life is not easy to draw. In the age of absolutism (as in Denmark in the first part of the nineteenth century) there was, at least in principle, a stable sphere of public life that was given to citizens to be active within. Matters of State were reserved to those who were born or called to such things. In a democratic era, the sphere of public life is not defined in the same way. The respective rights and obligations of individuals, corporations, and governments are in a state of perpetual flux, and political activity is implicit in any decision as to where a particular form of life is to be located. In an age of revolution, the Assessor's view that a man should enter a profession is questionable in a way that is not so in an age lived under the premises of stability and sempiternal order. In an age of radical autonomy, the idea of vocation loses its rationale, and individuals are not drawn to pre-existing roles but engage in a constant redefinition of roles. In this regard, much of what Kierkegaard could view as belonging to the life of a private citizen, without political implications, is transformed, and becomes, at least indirectly, political. Food, gender, literature—everything is now, in a sense, "political." In this perspective, even the urbane Johannes Climacus, smoking his cigar in Frederiksberg Gardens and watching the working world (from which he abstains) pass by, even he is making a "political" statement. But this is by our standards, not Kierkegaard's. If we live in a late stage of this development, he stands at its dawn and in this regard the paradox is that it is precisely in Kierkegaard's quest for an authentically Christian existence that he pioneers just this transformation of the political.

With these comments on urbanity, citizenship and the political in mind let us return to Arendt's metaphorical definition of the political as stepping forward so as to enter the domain of public discourse—not metaphorical for ancient Athenians, of course, but in our age of mass communication an image that can no longer be taken in a direct or literal sense.

Stepping Forward in Character

The metaphor of stepping forward is essentially theatrical, itself a key Kierkegaardian category. To step forward into the public sphere is to make a dramatic entrance, to appear before others in the role by which one chooses to be defined—in life and for life. Whether we regard this political stage cynically as a theatre of ambition or more generously as the only milieu in which we can indeed "make a difference" may be open to debate—but this entanglement of the political with the theatrical is, I think, crucial to understanding what is going on with Kierkegaard in these years.

Now it is less a question of the aesthetic and the ethical as a question for the individual about the individual and more a matter of the aesthetic and the ethical qua forms of social existence.

We can pinpoint the issues in a couple of journal entries from, respectively, 1849 and 1851. From 1849: "What has shaken me again and again and what continues to shake me despite all my religious efforts is this thing of stepping forward in the character of author in such a way as to subject [myself] to a certain standard for an extended period perhaps for my whole life" (KJN 6: NB 11, 122, translation amended). And, from 1851, speaking of how Christianity's idea requires separation from the People's Church, "to undertake this separation is such a qualitatively religious act that only someone of qualitatively distinguished religious character can do it; strictly speaking, it would require an apostle, at the least a witness to the truth. And it must be done in character ... Now, I have not discovered one single person on our stage who could even bear a resemblance to such a distinguished religious character " (KJN 8: NB 24: 51, 351). Later in that same entry, Kierkegaard will put the question to himself as to whether he should "step forward as the person who, so to speak, has orders from God to reduce Xndom in rank? Oh, no. I am without authority." Looking back on the year 1848, however, Kierkegaard will in 1853 admit that he was for a moment tempted to believe that he was the superior Christian. It was immediately clear to him, however, that "if I really was the superior one, then it would be required of me to step forward in character in such a way that I would be ready to live in poverty and suffer in a different sense from what I had previously thought" (KJN 9: NB 28, 54).

In this perspective, the struggle of the late 1840s is a kind of repetition of the earlier struggle between the aesthetic and the ethical. There too, we recall, the issue could be represented as the struggle between the desire to live in a kind of secret shadow-world and a readiness to take up one's role in society. There too, this could be expressly figured in theatrical images. The Seducer is described as inhabiting a kind of stage behind the stage: "Through a hanging of fine gauze, one sees, as it were, a world of gauze, lighter, more ethereal, with a quality different from that of the actual world" (EO 1, 306). Conversely, as Constantin Constantius explains, the true office of theatrical art is, by focusing us on the possibilities represented on stage, to prepare us for the roles we must assume when we leave the shadow-world of the theatre and go out into the bright light of social life (FT/R, 154-5).

Yet it might seem that the first pseudonymous authorship itself, together with the accompanying upbuilding discourses, gets no further than a kind of hidden inwardness. The person who practices hidden inwardness has been freed from the compulsive self-deception and self-concealment of the aesthete. Applying the metaphor of stepping forward, such a one has stepped from the darkness of self-ignorance into the light of repentant self-knowledge and is transfigured in the light of the divine presence. Nevertheless, even in the moment of transfiguration such a person remains invisible to the world. But in the second half of the 1840s it seems that it is no longer enough to humble ourselves in nothingness before God in the passion of inwardness. Now, it seems, the Christian must become visible and bear witness to the world, in the world.

What does this witness involve? Love, certainly. Yet though love is known by its fruits, there is no work of love that can ever appear in the world unambiguously. Every apparent work of love is interpretable as something else. Again the *Corsair* affair provides a telling example, since what Kierkegaard had regarded as a well-intentioned service to literary civility was cruelly misrepresented as extreme vanity. For this reason he would describe his treatment at the hands of *The Corsair* as a "martyrdom of laughter" (COR, xxx;

JP 2: 2046; JP 6: 6348). The entertainment offered by this particular one-act comedy belonged more to the theatre of cruelty than to the music-hall.

Even if it culminated in a kind of martyrdom, then, was this an example of the kind of stepping-forward in character that we have heard Kierkegaard proposing to himself? There are reasons to think not. As we have seen, Kierkegaard himself seems to have seen the affair as a "police action," which implies that it was conducted within the parameters of a given social and indeed secular order. In other words, it did not involve testimony to the qualitatively different order of justice to which we might imagine Christian witness appealing. Even within the social order of Copenhagen itself, the confrontation with rabble-barbarism belonged essentially to the gutter rather than the forum. At the same time, the fact that his opponents shielded themselves behind the anonymity denounced in *Two Ages* and that his own involvement was entangled with the pseudonymous persona of Frater Taciturnus meant that the affair lacked the aspect of "character" that belongs by definition to the idea of stepping forward in character. To this consideration we might add that since this idea also involves the person having a full understanding of what is at stake and that Kierkegaard seems not to have anticipated the scale of insult and obloquy that would be heaped upon him by the *Corsair*, his action in this case cannot count as stepping forward in a radically Christian sense. Finally, we may simply note that the explicit reflections on whether he should step forward in character post-date the *Corsair* affair. To the extent that Kierkegaard learnt from this affair what the cost of authentic Christian witness might potentially be it undoubtedly contributed to the development of his idea of such witness, but to be a witness to the truth in the most radical sense is something else again.

Here we pause to note two aspects of Kierkegaard's notion of being "in character." Firstly, it is primarily applied to his relation to his own authorship, being "in character as author," Here, the task is to bring about a relationship of responsibility and transparency, to communicate "directly" regarding the issue that is of ultimate concern to the author himself and in this way to be present in what is written as the character that the author chooses to be. Secondly, it acquires a very distinctive form when the character to be developed and lived up to is not the author's self-invented persona but the character demanded by Christianity.

Now it is not a secret that in these years Kierkegaard comes more and more to see discipleship as requiring the imitation of the suffering and crucified Christ. In this case, then, we are dealing not with a character invented by any human author but a prototypical character held up for imitation and assumption by all. Strikingly, the life of the one to be imitated also follows the movement from hiddenness to appearance that is demanded of the would-be follower. In the "Life of Christ" sketched in *Judge for Yourself*, Kierkegaard describes how "He belonged to nothing and to no one, was in no alliance with anything or with anybody, was a stranger in this world, in poverty and lowliness, without a nest, without a den, without a place where he could lay his head. Just like a straight line that touches the circle at only one point, so was he in the world and yet outside the world, serving only one master" (JFY, 167).[5] But this, as Kierkegaard immediately explains, is precisely a life of hidden inwardness: "he could have gone on living this way in quiet obscurity; his life could have become a secret worship in which he belonged, and totally belonged, to one master until death finally came" (JFY, 167). However, such a secret life would have fallen short of the task bestowed on him by God: to serve only one master. "[B]ut he wanted to make it known in the

[5] The image of the tangent is one that would be exploited by Karl Barth in his Commentary on Romans.

world, and that is why he had to step out on the stage of the human race, if I may so phrase it, in such a way that he could fasten, if possible, everyone's attention upon himself" (JFY, 168). But it is precisely this act of stepping forward that sets in motion the events that culminate on Calvary.

The character that Christians are to imitate and to make their own is, then, the character of one who actualizes the ideal by stepping forward onto the stage of human affairs, ready to endure all that will befall them as a result. But what does this mean for Kierkegaard? We have seen that, for Arendt, stepping forward is not a matter of "direct action" but of speech. Of course, Arendt knew perfectly well that our politics is no longer a face-to-face matter, as in ancient Athens. Our speech is and must be mediated in multiple ways. The most obvious of these—in Kierkegaard's time, at least—was writing. To write and to publish is, precisely, to make a public appearance, to be—or to become—a public voice. In this sense Kierkegaard is entirely justified over against those critics who say he never actually did anything, he just wrote. "Just writing" is never just writing. Writing is to enter public life. But then the whole tension between pseudonymity and stepping forward in character comes once more to the fore, since the question now concerns who one is to appear as in one's writing.

The issue is in some ways well-stated in a 1934 article by Alfred Bauemler, who says that, along with Nietzsche, Kierkegaard was one of the only two men of the 19th century who *acted*—but this action is, precisely, his writing: "*The Moment* is Kierkegaard's act and is to be understood entirely as praxis. [In it] Kierkegaard sacrifices himself."[6] There is much to disagree with in Bauemler's article, not least its overall political views, but it helps us to nuance

[6] Alfred Bauemler, 'Gedanken über Kierkegaard' in *Nationalsozialistische Monatshefte* 49 (1934),. 84.

the applicability of Arendt's view of political action to Kierkegaard.

Kierkegaard didn't have to give speeches on the hustings in order to act politically. He had only to do what he did best: to write. But to write was not, after all, so simple. As I have argued elsewhere, Kierkegaard saw the expansion of literary and journalistic publishing in the nineteenth century as a constant lure to the "chatter" of premise-authors and the dangers of anonymity.[7] Literature reveals a lure implicit in language itself. Annihilating the immediacy of pre-human life, language places us in a realm of open possibilities and, in doing so, confronts us with our essential responsibility for whatever we say, which is also responsibility for who we are. Anxiety beckons.

In this situation, to step forward in character as a Christian writer it is not enough simply to enunciate Christian propositions or positions. If we think that, we have succumbed to finitude. On the other hand, to imagine writing as absolutely creative is to lose oneself in a Romantic fantasy world. The task of the Christian writer is not simply to write about Christianity but in writing to show the possibility of free dependence on God. It is such a free dependence that Kierkegaard models in *The Point of View*, a work in which he attempts to mould the character, at once literary and religious, creative and obedient, in which he will be able to step out. For such a character, writing (the labor of attempting to write "christianly") is itself stepping out, with the emphasis on the present participial form of "writing." In the complex, differentiated, and reflective world of modernity, one way of being a Christian witness is to be, quite simply, a writer. Writing is itself a kind of existence. The fact that innumerable writers perished or suffered

---

[7] See George Pattison, *Kierkegaard and the Theology of the Nineteenth Century. The Paradox and the Point of Contact* (Cambridge: Cambridge University Press, 2012), 188-9.

persecution under the various tyrannical regimes of the twentieth century indicates that this is not an empty claim. To write, really to write, to write as who one is, "in character," is to step forward and take up a position within the public sphere. To do this necessarily involves exposure to manifold forms and degrees of both civil and uncivil, even violent, criticism (as anyone who has ever spoken out on any major issue of public concern will know). In Kierkegaard's case, stepping forward involved testimony to the claims of Christianity and therefore entailed the further claim that Christianity had a legitimate presence within the public life of the polis, although that presence was distorted and falsified when it was colonized as an organ of nation or state. It is perhaps open to discussion whether, as Bauemler thought, *The Moment* fully achieved testimony of this kind or whether the fact that, in the end, Kierkegaard could only publish *The Point of View* posthumously means that it remained an elusive desideratum. Either way, we may conclude that if we are to find a kind of political action properly describable as "Kierkegaardian," then it will be in the very act of writing, the movement from pen to paper to print to public that we must look.

Can There Be a Kierkegaardian Politics of Love?

Lee C. Barrett

The nature of Kierkegaard's political ethic, or even the question of whether he had one or not, has been a vexing puzzle for his readers ever since his writings first hit the press. This perplexity should not be surprising, for his texts on almost any subject are so multi-layered and polysemic that they can support radically divergent interpretations. Moreover, Kierkegaard's reflections on political matters are particularly supportive of diverse construals, for they are scattered, suggestive rather than exhaustive, ad hoc rather than systematic, riddled with irony, and seem to have evolved during the composition of his authorship. In light of such considerations, Bartholomew Ryan has recently argued that Kierkegaard's use of indirect communication destabilizes the reader's ideological commitments and communal loyalties, and thereby makes a plethora of political appropriations of his work inevitable.[1]

But even by the standards of Kierkegaard scholarship, the variety of interpretations of Kierkegaard's politics is stunning. Some

[1] Bartholomew Ryan, *Kierkegaard's Indirect Politics* (New York: Rodopi, 2014).

expositors have found him to be essentially and necessarily apolitical, utterly devoid of anything remotely like a socio-political ethic. For example, Martin Buber argued that Kierkegaard's privileging of the individual's solitary relationship with God rendered human sociality and its public institutions inessential to human flourishing.[2] Similarly, Theodor Adorno contended that Kierkegaard's focus on the interiority of love and on its motivational purity, rather than on love's actual consequences in the social world, generated an otherworldly indifference to the successful amelioration of the neighbor's political and economic woes.[3] In these depictions of the other-worldly, acosmic Kierkegaard, the Dane's focus on the transformation of the individual's purely internal attitudes, and his refusal to identify love with any specific set of external actions, could at most lead to a purely abstract and apolitical affirmation of the other.

Other interpreters, many of whom were often quite popular and influential, have discerned implicit political implications in Kierkegaard's authorship, but have concluded that he was some variety of conservative traditionalist whose political proclivities were epitomized in his criticisms of the revolution of 1848.[4] Some declared him to be an unqualified monarchist, suspicious of populist mass movements, who subscribed to a Lutheran "two kingdoms" view that severed the political realm of law from the spiritual realm of grace. After all, Kierkegaard did write in his "Open Letter to Dr. A. G. Rudelbach" in 1851, "There is nothing about

---

[2] Martin Buber, "The Question of the Single One," in *Between Man and Man* (New York: Macmillan, 1965), 52-65.

[3] Theodor Adorno, "On Kierkegaard's Doctrine of Love," *Studies in Philosophy and Social Science* 8 (1940): 413-29. See also Theodor Adorno, *Kierkegaard: Construction of the Aesthetic*, trans. Robert Hullot-Kentor (Minneapolis: University of Minnesota Press, 1989).

[4] See Walter Lowrie, *A Short Life of Kierkegaard* (Princeton: Princeton University Press, 1942).

which I have greater misgivings than about all that even slightly tastes of the disastrous confusion of politics and Christianity" (COR, 53). He continued, "…I am positive that I have never directed one word against the teaching and the organization of the established order," after having sharply distinguished Christian inwardness from the outward institutions of the political realm (Ibid, 56). More tragically (and more bizarrely), the Austrian jurist Carl Schmitt and the German theologian Emanuel Hirsch claimed to detect a justification for the leap into fascism and authoritarianism in Kierkegaard's valorization of decisive commitments and in his critique of bourgeois complacency and mediocrity.[5] Ironically, a similar appeal to Kierkegaard's alleged radical decisionism was used by Georg Lukács to overcome his lingering reservations about Marxism and to legitimate his embrace of Bolshevism.[6] So, perhaps Kierkegaard was a proto-fascist, or perhaps he was a proto-Stalinist.

On the other hand, some interpreters have discovered a more liberal, anti-elitist, anti-traditionalist, and anti-totalitarian Kierkegaard. As early as 1961 Jørgen Bukdahl described Kierkegaard as a champion of the common man, and therefore as the enemy of the cultural dynamics of elitism.[7] In the last three decades Kierkegaard scholars like Merold Westphal have argued that Kierkegaard's critique of totalizing philosophical systems functioned in part as an exposé of the self-deification of any political culture.[8]

---

[5] Carl Schmitt, *Political Theology*, trans. George Schwab (Chicago: University of Chicago Press, 2005); Emanuel Hirsch, *Kierkegaard-Studien*, 3 vols. (Gütersloh: Bertelsmann, 1930-33) vol. 3, 909-956.

[6] See Arpad Kadarkay, *Georg Lukács: Life, Thought, and Politics* (Oxford: Blackwell, 1991), 193-225.

[7] Jørgen Bukdahl, *Kierkegaard and the Common Man*, trans. Bruce H. Kirmmse (Grand Rapids: Eerdmans, 2001).

[8] Merold Westphal, *Kierkegaard's Critique of Reason and Society* (University Park: Pennsylvania State University Press, 1991).

According to Westphal's reading of Kierkegaard, conceptualities that promise closure have an elective affinity with collectivities that claim ultimacy. Mark Dooley, following the lead of Derrida and John Caputo, portrays Kierkegaard as an ideological liminal person, an émigré, the implacable enemy of all political meta-narratives.[9] In a more restricted way, Bruce Kirmmse has contended that Kierkegaard in his later years came to endorse the liberal dissolution of the synthesis of church and state, and that his sympathies lay with the peasant reform movement.[10] Somewhat similarly, Stephen Backhouse has discovered a virulently anti-nationalist Kierkegaard.[11] Eliseo Pérez-Álvarez has even claimed to discover the seeds of liberation theology's economic analysis in Kierkegaard's later works.[12]

Robert Perkins' life work has much in common with this last group of Kierkegaard scholars. Like them, he too saw that Kierkegaard's authorial project had profound implications for the political realm. However, Perkins' interpretation had a particular and unique slant. Even more than his colleagues, he based his investigation of Kierkegaard's political sensibilities on Kierkegaard's treatment of certain religious and moral virtues and vices, such as envy.[13] For example, Perkins argued that in Kierkegaard's pages

---

[9] Mark Dooley, *The Politics of Exodus* (New York: Fordham University Press, 2001).

[10] Bruce H. Kirmmse, *Kierkegaard in Golden Age Denmark* (Bloomington: Indiana University Press, 1990).

[11] Stephen Backhouse, *Kierkegaard's Critique of Christian Nationalism* (Oxford: Oxford University Press, 2011.

[12] Eliseo Pérez-Álvarez, *A Vexing Gadfly: The Late Kierkegaard on Economic Matters* (Eugene, OR: Pickwick, 2009).

[13] Robert L. Perkins, "Envy as Personal Phenomenon and as Politics," in *International Kierkegaard Commentary: Two Ages*, ed. Robert L. Perkins (Macon: Mercer University Press, 1984), 107-132. See also Robert L. Perkins, "Kierkegaard's Anti-Climacus in His Social and Political Environment," in *International Kierkegaard Commentary: Practice*

certain political and cultural formations make envy more likely and more virulent than in others. This essay will follow the trail blazed by Perkins, seeking clues for Kierkegaard's political sensibilities in his exposition of Kierkegaard's preeminent virtue, love for the neighbor.

It must be admitted right away that a massive problem haunts any such effort to derive a politics from Kierkegaard's treatment of love. The problem is this: Is there any strong rationale in Kierkegaard's authorship for trying to improve the life of the neighbor by attempting to change the neighbor's political and economic situation? Or does love for the neighbor exclusively manifest itself as concern for the neighbor's spiritual growth, which is quite independent of all material conditions? The problem arises through the conjunction of two different themes that permeate Kierkegaard's works. That conjunction occurs most vividly and dramatically in *Works of Love*.

The first theme is Kierkegaard's often repeated conviction that the attainment of a loving disposition is the *telos* of human life. An individual's love for the neighbor is nothing less than a redoubling of the love which is the very life of God, a reflection of God's extravagant love for humanity (WL, 64-65). Consequently, the pursuit of a life of radical love for the neighbor is the absolute good that should be prioritized over all lesser goods. The goods of longevity, political enfranchisement, familial felicity, and the possession of material resources pale by comparison. Kierkegaard insists that this love for the neighbor is inherently other-regarding and is a genuine concern for the well-being of the other (Ibid, 83). Genuine love does not dwell on itself and does not admire its own virtue. For Kierkegaard, the neighbor, this other to be loved, is not humanity in the abstract, but is the concrete, individuated other,

---

in Christianity, ed. Robert L. Perkins (Macon: Mercer University Press, 2004) 274-302.

with specific needs. Furthermore, this love is active rather than passive; it expresses itself through works. Although the hidden source of love in the inner being of God cannot be discerned, love must strive to become recognizable through its fruits (Ibid, 14). So far, given all these considerations, it would seem that Kierkegaard's emphasis of active attention to the concrete needs of the neighbor would mandate political action to better meet the particular needs of the particular neighbor, in so far as the satisfaction of the neighbor's needs are related to social, economic, and political factors.

But another prominent theme in *Works of Love* must be taken into account. According to Kierkegaard, what the neighbor really needs is the same thing that the lover of the neighbor needs: to grow in love. The neighbor's telos is the same as the lover's telos. Therefore, what all our neighbors need most decisively is to become more loving. So, to love one's neighbor in obedience to the biblical commandment most essentially involves "building up" love in that neighbor. Put simply, to love another person is to help that person grow in love (Ibid, 107, 114, 121, 130). Kierkegaard identifies "building up love" in another with helping that individual to stand alone before God, attain spiritual independence from the "crowd's" tranquilizing potencies, and to develop the capacity to make a life-shaping commitment to a policy of love. Kierkegaard adds the crucial point that the neighbor can also be helped by another person to become sensitized to God's gift of love for her unique self, for that is the source of all growth in love.

The problem arises when Kierkegaard adds the claim that in regard to the cultivation of a life of love, the neighbor's political situation may not be very important, or possibly not significant at all. Kierkegaard describes the highest good, the life of love, as being independent of all lesser goods, like physical health or material prosperity. Paralleling the Kantian mantra that "ought" implies "can," Kierkegaard claims that the equality of the obligation to love implies an equality of ability. For Kierkegaard, the universality of the love commandment cannot be jeopardized by adverse social circumstances. In this vein Kierkegaard frequently asserts that the freedom to love is impervious to necessitating conditions. The radically free individual's capacity to love cannot be decisively harmed by environmental factors, including political and economic ones. The command "You shall love" admits of no exceptions and tolerates no privileged positions on the spectrum of material resources and political power. Kierkegaard insists that the imperative "shall" is blessedly independent of all worldly contingencies (Ibid, 391). When it comes to the one thing that makes life worth living, the pursuit of a life of love, the rich and powerful have no advantage over the poor and marginalized. Neither poverty nor oppression can destroy or decisively harm the neighbor's ability to love, for the capacity to love is radically independent of the neighbor's material well-being.

Putting these two themes together, the conclusion would seem to be that one's primary obligation is to help the neighbor grow in love, and that obligation does not involve concern for the improvement of the neighbor's social and political situation. The neighbor can grow in love with or without a job, with or without the right to vote, and with or without adequate medical care. If this conclusion is valid it would seem to legitimate sociopolitical passivity and even indifference to the neighbor's material misery and oppression. Perhaps Adorno and Buber were right about Kierkegaard after all.

Many portions of *Works of Love* do seem to support this conclusion. In that text Kierkegaard emphatically asserts that Christianity does not seek to tamper with the worldly distinctions of status and position. He remarks, "...with the calmness of eternity it [Christianity] surveys equably all the distinctions of earthly life but does not decisively take sides with any single one" (Ibid, 70). He advises his reader, "Do not busy yourself with changing the shape of the world or your situation, as if you...instead of being a poor charwoman, perhaps could manage to be called 'Madame'" (Ibid, 136). Kierkegaard insists that advancement in social status and the relative prestige of different social roles will all be forgotten in eternity (Ibid, 87). These remarks may sound like a laudable subversion of classism or an antidote to an inordinate longing for upward mobility. But Kierkegaard's insouciance about social class is extended to more basic economic realities. The "world," and by that he means the superficial and sinful world, may feel obliged to attempt to remediate the misfortunes of the poor, but that endeavor is misguided, for the cultivation of inwardness is vastly more important than money or hospitals (Ibid, 324). It certainly sounds like the poor should be content with their miserable lot, and that they should be exhorted to accept their plight.

Further, Kierkegaard also warns that participation in zealous political action can divert the individual's attention away from humanity's ultimate good. He excoriates the inflated promises of political reform movements, for no political program can resolve the most crucial problems in human life (Ibid, 70). Political ideologies, he warns, cannot produce felicity. Mass reform movements shift the focus away from the individual's own subjectivity and tempt her to lose herself in the crowd. The individual is distracted from her fundamental task of personal transformation and becomes obsessed with the hoped-for world-historical consequences of political action. Even worse, in order to be effective all political projects require corporate action, and that necessity for co-operation entices the malleable individual to relinquish her personal responsibility to the faceless crowd.

Given this plethora of passages, it would seem that Kierkegaard, or at least the implied author of *Works of Love*, really was apolitical. The one thing needful, building up love in the neighbor, does not require attention to the political realities in which the neighbor's life is embedded. After all, the neighbor can grow in love even if the neighbor is suffering from unjust imprisonment or has no access to health care.

But Kierkegaard's texts are always too multi-layered and multi-vocal to sustain such a one-dimensional conclusion. *Works of Love* is animated by other dynamics that suggest that economic and political circumstances and institutional structures can indeed impinge upon the ability to love and the duty to build up love in the neighbor. If this is so, then the duty to build up love in the neighbor would include a duty to work for the improvement of the neighbor's political and economic circumstances.

Most obviously, Kierkegaard was not oblivious to the psychical-sensate dimension of the ability to love. The neighbor cannot grow in love if the neighbor is cognitively debilitated, volitionally incapacitated by illness, or dead. According to Kierkegaard, the sensate-psychical aspects of life are the necessary substratum, the precondition, for growth in love (Ibid, 209). For Kierkegaard, these preconditions include the psychological capacity for self-consciousness, volition, and intentional action. The crucial consideration here is that the distribution and availability of the goods that make these things possible are dependent on societal institutions and dynamics. An inadequacy of food supplies, medical care, etc. could jeopardize the ability to love. Although Kierkegaard is quick to point out that physical well-being should never be regarded as an end-in-itself, he recognized that at least minimal physical well-being is the substructure for all growth in love.

The recommendation that we should strive to keep our neighbors alive may not seem to be a very exciting qualification of the notion that to love the neighbor is to help the neighbor to grow in love. Of course, we might say, the love commandment implies that one should help keep the neighbor alive and at least minimally functional. And, of course some economic and political systems might promote that survival of the neighbor more than others. But Kierkegaard sometimes hints at a more robust and productive reason for engaging in political action. The reason is this: the lover of the neighbor may be called upon to resist specific impediments to the neighbor's growth in love, and these impediments may include factors that go far beyond the requisites for simple biological survival.

Kierkegaard often writes as if some societal circumstances unnecessarily make growth in love more difficult for the neighbor than it need be. Most of these are instances of adverse socialization that encourage the individual to "forget God" (Ibid, 127). Certain patterns of communal life reinforce the sinful tendency toward unloving selfishness, or at least shape that proclivity in particularly pernicious ways that are difficult to remediate. Some of these patterns that are condemned by Kierkegaard are micro-social practices. For example, he observes that parents encourage an inordinate love of money in their children by not going to church in order to evade the duty to contribute to the church's maintenance and mission (Ibid, 320-21). Children subjected to such crass parental examples of selfish behavior will have to struggle harder than their peers to resist the temptations of greed.

Kierkegaard has even more critical things to say about macro-social practices. Many of these practices, he laments, encourage cultural snobbery and classism, phenomena that discourage the alleged elites from loving their social inferiors, and inhibit the alleged inferiors' ability to see their own efforts to grow in love as having much value. Those who are routinely treated with contempt have a difficult time believing in their own power to effect meaningful change, including their power to assume responsibility for the direction of their own lives. Moreover, the whole edifice of classicism functions as an exercise of social control, and for Kierkegaard control is inimical to respecting the general freedom of the other, of which the freedom to love is a subset. Kierkegaard cautions that the cunning and often devious behavior of financiers who trade in commodities fosters a fear of being deceived and a generalized suspicion of one's neighbors (Ibid, 238). In *Two Ages* Kierkegaard had similarly castigated the present age's fear of being duped, its prudential caution, and its tendency to be "strangled by calculation" (TA, 68). This makes it exceedingly difficult to presuppose that the seed of love exists in the other, something that the upbuilding of the other in love requires (WL, 216-22). It is hard to discern your neighbor's potential to love if society has taught you that your neighbor is always looking for new ways to cheat you. Moreover, mass journalism habitually attempts to increase circulation by purveying slander, which puts further obstacles in the path of cultivating neighbor love in oneself or others. Defamatory slander encourages people to see one another as nothing but scoundrels and obscures the seed of love implanted in every individual. Sadly, Kierkegaard concludes, the world of business is structured so that "calculating sagacity," greed, and selfishness will be rewarded (Ibid, 260).

Many of the societal dynamics that Kierkegaard condemns were the standard operating procedures of early modern capitalism and nascent mass communication. They were structural issues, produced by a specific social configuration, that of modernity. Kierkegaard observed that the spirit of modernity was communicated not only though commonly shared concepts, but also through psychical-sensate vehicles, or, as we would say, through material conditions and institutional practices. Here Kierkegaard implicitly recognizes that different social arrangements and different cultural sensibilities generate different impediments to the growth of love in oneself and in the neighbor. If this is so, then it would be an act of love for the neighbor, aimed at building up love in the neighbor, to struggle to remove those systemic impediments.

Kierkegaard had already explored this cultural variability of the forms of sin a year earlier in his literary review of the novel *Two Ages*. There he emphasized the differences between the age of revolution and the contemporary age (TA, 60-112). Both ages possessed dynamics that militated against the development of authentic human life and relationships, but the dynamics were different in each one and the malformations of the human spirit were different. The revolutionary age encouraged an impetuosity that reacted against the restrains of tradition, while the contemporary age fosters a debilitating reflectiveness and a cautious and superficial pragmatism. Although neither was conducive to the flourishing of genuine love for the neighbor (Kierkegaard did have more positive things to say about the passion of the age of revolution), the important point is that the impediments that they placed in the path of love were different and were historically contingent. If these variables are contingent and variable, then they could be resisted and reformed.

But even these considerations might not by themselves justify a type of Kierkegaardian political action. One could conclude that, even granted Kierkegaard's recognition of all this cultural variability in the impediments to love, he was only writing to encourage his readers to inwardly combat the deleterious influence of the social order upon their own souls. Perhaps he was suggesting: retreat inward and just say "No" to such ideologies as classism. If so, the solution to the problem would be the transformation of the individual's subjectivity, and not a transformation of politic structures. Perhaps Kierkegaard was only advocating for efforts to change the individual, and not efforts to change the system.

As always, Kierkegaard's writings are more complex than such an analysis would suggest. There are trajectories in *Works of Love* that do point toward a more vigorous activism aimed at reforming the socio-political system. For example, concerning practices that buttress class prestige, Kierkegaard warns that "the relationships among human beings ought and never may be such that the one worships and the other is the one worshipped" (WL, 125). He calls for a visible non-participation in the social practices that reinforce classism, and exhorts that one's life should be a rebuke to those who support it (Ibid, 127). Kierkegaard writes, "Even if you say nothing, he [one's classist friend] no doubt notices that your life, if it truly relates to God's requirement, contains an admonition, a requirement for him" (Ibid, 127). This opposition would be active, publicly observable, and could lead to a weakening of the institutionalized structures that reinforce classism. Of course, Kierkegaard was not advocating for a boycott of private dining clubs, or a legislative initiative to ban them, but he was implicitly recommending an active non-compliance with deleterious social practices. Such a public witness would be a form of resistance to the social system, and therefore would be a political act aimed at societal reform. Kierkegaard was inching toward the politics of non-cooperation with spirit-destroying cultural regimes, a politics that was familiar to radical Pietists and Anabaptists.

So far, Kierkegaard's interest in the structures and dynamics of public life seem to be restricted to those factors that can inhibit growth in love. However, the project of building up love in the neighbor can do more than just resist the societal obstacles to the flourishing of love. Kierkegaard implies that action in the public sphere can attempt something much more daring: it can aspire to upbuild the neighbor through changing the neighbor's circumstances. In some instances a change of structural environmental factors can positively foster growth in love.

Here a critical consideration that must be kept in mind is Kierkegaard's analysis of the limitations on what one person can do for another in the upbuilding of love. He insists that love must be freely given in order to count as genuine love. Consequently, building up the neighbor in love cannot be achieved through compulsion or seduction. Love can only be invited by another human, but it can never be coerced. Kierkegaard insists that, in order to preserve the neighbor's responsible agency, love can only be drawn forth from the neighbor through maieutic means. Therefore, the neighbor's confidence in her own ability to choose, which is a precondition for choosing the life of love, must be encouraged. The elicitation of the neighbor's confidence in her ability to choose, and her self-assumption of responsibility, can be promoted by exhibiting trust in her volitional capacities. That trust cannot be demonstrated solely by words, but must be embodied in concrete acts and social practices, by "behavior in everyday affairs" (Ibid, 213). Accordingly, Kierkegaard insists that the poor should not be treated condescendingly, as if their economic circumstances prevented them from performing acts of mercy and love. He castigates the cultural adoration of the beneficence of the wealthy, for that can induce a "false shame" in the poor, and convince them that they lack the ability to be merciful and charitable (Ibid, 322-330). The celebration of charitable donations by the rich, such as naming public buildings after them, undermines the confidence of the poor in the power of their own moral agency. However, by treating the poor as responsible agents, and by fostering social practices that give them confidence in their capacity to make life-shaping choices, the precondition for choosing a life of love can be built up. Although Kierkegaard does not draw this conclusion in *Works of Love,* such encouragement of the neighbor's volitional capacities could be promoted through the neighbor's political enfranchisement. Here Kierkegaard plants a seed for an argument against all paternalistic and authoritarian political regimes.

Yet another trajectory concerning the possibility of building up love in the neighbor through political means is evident in *Works of Love.* For Kierkegaard, human love is a response to God's love. But God's love is not directly perceived; it becomes indirectly visible, at least in part, through human works of love. Consequently, the neighbor can be upbuilt in love by receiving love from other humans. Kierkegaard reminds his reader that such human love for the neighbor must express itself in embodied contexts, including the responsibilities of particular political relationships. Kierkegaard is clear that this upbuilding love that expresses and reflects God's love can be manifested through the solicitous discharging of social obligations and roles. These role-specific obligations do include concern for the other's material well-being. Kierkegaard cites the example of a parent's concern for the well-being of her child (Ibid, 214). By diligently providing for her family, a parent's love is expressed in deeds rather than merely in words. By analogy, political action aimed at improving the neighbor's material circumstances could be an enactment of a solicitude that, if perceived as motivated by love, could upbuild the neighbor in love.

So, does Kierkegaard work at cross-purposes with himself? On the one hand, the love that should be built up in the neighbor is supposed to be independent of environmental influences. On the other hand, certain political configurations work against the upbuilding of love, and certain forms of political action may contribute to the upbuilding of love. The first trajectory tends to minimize the importance of political action on behalf of the neighbor, while the second trajectory seems to require it.

Perhaps Kierkegaard is not indulging in an egregious self-contradiction here. Even in one volume he may be writing to two different implied audiences and may be pursuing two different rhetorical and edifying purposes. These different audiences are not necessarily different sets of people, for different aspects of any given individual may fall into both groups. To the disadvantaged and disenfranchised, or the disadvantaged and disenfranchised dimension of anyone, Kierkegaard's good news is that they can still do the one thing needful for human flourishing: they can still love the neighbor. No amount of oppression can deprive them of that. However, for those with some social power and political agency, or those dimensions of anyone who enjoys such power, Kierkegaard's exhortation is that the effort to upbuild love in the neighbor includes the imperative to remove societal impediments to the growth of love, and the imperative to exemplify love through concern for the neighbor's material well-being. For example, anyone with any modicum of social capital should use it to resist classism and anything else that puts a stumbling block in the neighbor's path. Some of Kierkegaard's remarks are directed to those who fear that they do not have the resources or the opportunity to love their neighbor, and other remarks are directed to those who need instruction in the concrete ways to love the neighbor. How these two themes are to be integrated cannot be achieved through a theory of the relation of free-will to the power of the political environment; they can only be integrated in the messy hurly-burly of the particularities of an individual life.

A Response (and, Hopefully, a Little More)

Christopher A. P. Nelson

... For I was hungry and you gave me something to eat, I was thirsty and you gave me something to drink, I was a stranger and you invited me in, I needed clothes and you clothed me, I was sick and you looked after me, I was in prison and you came to visit me. —Matthew 25:34-36 (NIV)

Part I: A Symposium in Honor of Robert Perkins

In one of those "miscellaneous questions" chapters toward the end of the first Book of his *Nicomachean Ethics* (NE I:12), Aristotle wonders about the proper mode of comportment vis-à-vis the highest good, specifically, whether "honor" or "praise" is the more appropriate response to an object (or subject) of true wonder. Arguing for the former, Aristotle distinguishes between the two by proposing, basically, that honoring something (or someone) necessarily involves what we would call an existential dimension, while merely praising something (or someone) does not. Recognizing as well that, for Aristotle, admiration is essentially wonder with a subject as its object, it is in this spirit that I have attempted to compose this response to the papers that are contained in this volume.

To forestall any lingering concerns that I might lapse into mere praise—or worse, hagiography—I will begin by noting the three things that Bob and I disagreed about. The first two are, arguably, relatively minor concerns; the third, not so much.

Our first two disagreements (disagreements that we continued to jestingly resuscitate from time to time over the years) were occasioned by my first submission of an essay for consideration for inclusion in a volume of the *International Kierkegaard Commentary*. The volume was *IKC XX: Practice in Christianity*. Having recently completed some research at St. Olaf's for my doctoral dissertation, in which the character and writings of Anti-Climacus claimed pride of place, I was encouraged by Gordon Marino to submit something for this volume. In the letter that I later received from Robert L. Perkins, Editor, I learned that my essay was rejected. I took the liberty of responding to Dr. Perkins in turn, which occasioned a second letter from the Editor, in which he expressed that mine was the most gracious response to a rejection letter that he had ever seen. This was my first indication that here was an editor who probably cared at least as much about his authors, as he did about their words. I cannot remember the friendliness or the graciousness that occasioned Bob's friendly and gracious second correspondence; but I do remember the two things that I explicitly "stuck to my guns" about, even though they were identified as real "red flags" by the readers. First, while never mentioning him by name, Johannes de Silentio (author of *Fear and Trembling*) *does* identify Jesus as a "knight of faith." Second, there *is* something genuinely concerning about the proximity of the persona of Vigilius Haufniensis (author of *The Concept of Anxiety*) to the existential sphere of the "demonic." Neither of these disagreements was ever resolved; but that really doesn't matter, as they were fun disagreements to have.

Our third disagreement, however, was only gradually occasioned, and it was flavored more by gravity, than by levity. I am probably not alone in having had some form of this disagreement with Bob, namely, the disagreement about the very idea of there being a fruitful "political" dimension to Kierkegaard's work. I, for instance, would find (and do find) Ambrose Bierce's definition of the political to be of the "funny because it's true" variety:

> Politics, *n.* A strife of interests masquerading as a contest of principles. The conduct of public affairs for private advantage. (*The Devil's Dictionary*).

I'm laughing right now as I write this. I suspect that Bob would have a slightly different reaction. Because I never directly broached topics or themes in political philosophy in any of my writings, Bob and I never had the occasion to clash directly on this issue. But in hindsight, I can see that he was always pushing me away from my tacit, but apparently obvious (and to a large extent still rather common-place) assumption regarding the "apolitical Kierkegaard." This does not, of course, put me in any kind of privileged relationship with Bob—he pushed many of us in this way. Consider, for instance, the following passage from his "Introduction" to *IKC XVII: Christian Discourses* (a volume in which I had *two* submissions included):

> Both Marx and Kierkegaard worked very hard that frightfully decisive year [1848]. There are tremendous ironies here, for *The Communist Manifesto* and *Christian Discourses* look in opposite directions and can scarcely be compared. Those in the twentieth century who inherited and puzzled over their conflicting views left their conflicts unresolved, and that is perhaps the only lesson that can be learned by

> attempting to think about them in dialogue. *It is interesting that the contributors to this volume ignore the ambiguities of these close distant relations.* That both Kierkegaard and Marx rejected the justification offered on behalf of a bourgeois form of life in all its contemporary forms as humanly fulfilling is important. One sought revolution to achieve a new form of life in this world without transcendence; the other, in the tradition of the prophets, sought to establish the authority of the Unconditional (CD 4, emphasis added).

I cannot remember Bob ever having called out an entire group of *IKC* contributors like that (and having two contributions in the volume, I felt like he swatted me twice). Merold Westphal—about whom, more later—is perhaps the only contributor to this volume who might cry, "foul," inasmuch as he, unlike the rest of us, at least mentioned the name of "Marx," once, in passing.

This disagreement about the political dimension of Kierkegaard's work is also, as of yet, unresolved—witness, for instance, the five papers contained in this volume (not to mention the discussion set to ensue once I wrap this piece up). There are some deep disagreements here, and more than just a couple of positions to stake out in this regard. In the space I have left, I would like to briefly summarize what I have taken away from the contributions of Professors Davenport, Piety, Evans, Pattison, and Barrett—if only to begin to sketch out a map of the main lines of the terrain—and then to repay a little something on a debt long overdue.

Part II: Kierkegaard and Political Theology

Playing upon a neat ambiguity in the word, "profane"—which can and does mean a string of things from unholy, to secular, to vulgar, to debased, all with varying connotations—John Davenport argues that, while Kierkegaard may have swung the pendulum a bit too far in his final years, his "more balanced view" of the 'profanity' of politics is both appealing and entirely applicable to the politicking of our own day. Indeed, what Davenport finds especially disturbing is that and how Kierkegaard's critique of the inherent profanity of politics is even more applicable (and correspondingly more frightening) today than it was in Kierkegaard's own day. What was once, perhaps, merely a dangerous *distraction* from conscientious and independent ethical-religious decision-making and action, has now evolved into a positively *corruptive* force with the willful complicity of leaders in both (some) major mass media outlets and (some) major religious institutions. Trying to end on a positive note, however, Davenport suggests that "politics need not be this profane"—that "the inwardness thesis" and "the justice thesis" need not be construed as mutually exclusive—and proceeds to suggest reforms in education and mass media as possible antidotes to this devolution of politics. Such reforms, however, would almost certainly call for some concerted political action; and if our politics is already as profane as Davenport has (compellingly) argued, the prospects in that regard are not exactly promising.

Also playing upon a neat ambiguity, M.G. Piety proposes to investigate Kierkegaard's "apocryphal" politics. So, which is it: is there a Kierkegaardian politics hidden in his works, or is "Kierkegaardian politics" a 'work' that simply does not belong in his body of work properly construed and should therefore be discarded? Perhaps not surprisingly, it all depends on what you want to mean by "Kierkegaardian politics." At least two things, according to Piety, could be meant by this: (A) Kierkegaard's "expressly held political views, or (B) the political views that can be reasonably inferred from, or made to cohere with, his more general philosophical and theological views." On the first point, and arguing against a seeming legion of big names who would and have argued otherwise, Kierkegaard, according to Piety, is quite simply a monarchist, and he is so because he had more faith in the individual (who has an easier time listening to his or her conscience) than in any collective (which, the louder it gets, makes it harder and harder to hear anything but the chatter of the mob). On the second point, however, Piety is sympathetic to the idea that there are clearly inferable political views from Kierkegaard's general philosophical and theological views (irrespective of commitments to any particular form of government, or party alliance). Among them: the idea that ameliorating spiritual disorientation is not unrelated to ameliorating material poverty but is rather its motivating prerequisite; and the idea that the particular political contours of a city (or state, or nation, etc.) can in fact make it easier or more difficult to achieve this kind of amelioration (an idea that is revisited, pro and contra, by Barrett and Evans, respectively).

In his attempt to "put the modern [liberal] state in its place," C. Stephen Evans may be taken as a kind of arbiter between the positions staked out by Davenport and Piety (which is to say that both of them will find as much to disagree with as to agree with here). Evans begins by proposing that Kierkegaard's relative disinterest in political issues, specifically, is primarily a function of his excessive interest in another kind of issue altogether—i.e., the absolute, eternal, and essential (or what we might call 'the sacred'), as opposed to the relative, temporal, and contingent (or what we might call 'the profane'). For Kierkegaard, the former is of absolute importance, as opposed to the merely relative importance of the latter—and "politics," according to Evans, falls decidedly into this latter category. Thus, according to Evans, the true meaning and value of an individual human being's existence is entirely unrelated to the particular political reality in which he or she finds him or herself. This is not to say that politics is entirely irrelevant, but rather that it is decisively limited in importance. Neither is this to say that Kierkegaard has absolutely nothing to say that might prove politically fruitful—Evans proposes Kierkegaard's "faith in human equality" before God as a prime example and identifies some instances of Kierkegaard drawing out some of the relevant political implications of this faith himself. Still, in the end, the danger looms of being tempted to channel neighbor love simply or solely through political means—a temptation that, if succumbed to, according to Evans, could completely occlude the more fundamental calling to "love others in concrete ways in the particular circumstances of our daily lives."

In something of a departure from the rest of the panel, George Pattison effectively proposes to take a step back by querying what it is we want to mean by the word, "politics," in the first place—or, rather, how "politics" would have to be defined in order to characterize Kierkegaard's work as (in any way, shape, or form) "political." Drawing upon the writings of Hannah Arendt (who follows Aristotle in this respect), Pattison proposes a working definition of "politics" according to which the primary form of political action is "speaking," or "making a statement," in the sense of staking out a position, showing a way forward, or placing an obstacle in the way of some contrary "statement." Never mind having to infer political implications *from* Kierkegaard's writings, if this is our working definition of the "political"—staking out a position (by, e.g., shoring up on fronts aesthetic, ethical, theological, etc.), showing a way forward (rather than, e.g., merely ringing the alarm), or placing an obstacle in the way of some contrary statement (the business of much of Kierkegaard's work, early, middle, late, pseudonymous, and signed)—then Kierkegaard could arguably be construed as one of the most thoughtful and complicated "political" authors of all time. That "if," of course, is a really big "if," and some might worry that identifying "writing" with political action is a first step in an aesthetic retreat, not only from the political realm ('properly' conceived), but from the ethical-religious realm as well. To be sure, not every kind of "writing," or "stepping out," is an "act" in this sense—Pattison explicitly excludes the parroting of dogma, and romantic escapism, for instance; other kinds of writing could certainly be added to the list. And this is where

Pattison finds what I take to be his main question: Which, if any, of Kierkegaard's literary acts would actually fit the bill? The affair with the Corsair? Any of the pseudonymous works? The attack literature of the last years of his life? The posthumously published *Point of View*? It all depends on what it means to truly step forward "in character"—a question that, as Pattison rightly emphasizes, tended to haunt Kierkegaard throughout his career as an author. As a result, for my part, I would suggest the short little work, *On My Work as an Author*, as the best place to start.

In a fitting conclusion to this five-act play, Lee Barrett begins his exploration of love and politics by remarking, rightly, that the debate regarding "Kierkegaard and political theology" is a veritable free-for-all. With his own typical bold confidence, Barrett nevertheless enters the fray himself. Homing in on the one thing that all our authors/presenters have at least alluded to, regardless of what the particular argument may be about, if the argument is about Kierkegaard's work, then the centrality of the command to "love thy neighbor" simply cannot be ignored. Adopting this tacit consensus as his point of departure, Barrett asks, simply, whether there can be a "politics of love" (or, in an earlier draft, whether "love can be political"). Touching down again and again on issues raised and treated by Piety and Evans, Barrett poses what he takes to be the fundamental conundrum at the heart of the issue, thusly: (A) the command to love the neighbor obviously can (and does) mean to help the neighbor grow in spiritual love; (B) the command to love the neighbor obviously can (and does) mean to help the neighbor vis-à-vis the material conditions of his or her existence; and (C) construing the command in the first way tends to work at the expense of following the command in the second way, and vice-versa. Barrett's proposed solution to this conundrum? Kierkegaard may, at different times, be "writing to two different implied audiences and … pursuing two different rhetorical and edifying purposes." Whether or not this "both/and" gambit will satisfy any of the other participants in this debate, it does provide a neat segue to my brief concluding remarks.

Part III: Truth Is Subjectivity

I began this response with an account of my first correspondence with Robert Perkins. I think it is only fitting to conclude with an account of my last correspondence with Bob. After that first rejection letter, I managed to become a regular contributor to every successive volume of the *IKC*, and, for the last few volumes, to become a member of the series' Advisory Committee. The final volume in the series was *IKC 22: The Point of View*, in which I had two submissions included. In the second of these pieces, I was engaged in the project of arguing that the aborted "series of lectures on the dialectic of ethical and ethical-religious communication" begun in 1846 were not, contrary to the conventional view, abandoned in 1847, but that Kierkegaard continued to revisit and revise these notes up to the point at which he finally published *On My Work as an Author* (1851)—and that this was somehow an important recognition. I believe that I managed to make this case convincingly, but in the process, I found myself contending with a concept that is found nowhere else outside these notes—i.e., the concept of the "capability communication" (as opposed to a "knowledge communication"). I wrestled with this concept—trying to think it in terms of potentially cognate concepts (indirect communication, existence-communication, reduplication, revelation, etc.)—but, in the end, I resigned to conclude what Kierkegaard himself appears to have concluded: the concept either cannot, or should not, be made the object of direct discourse (or worse: that the concept itself was a dead-end, rightfully abandoned by its author). In the last substantive exchange that I had with Bob, he prodded me: "keep working on it; there's something there, and I know you can find it." This was Bob: always pushing me to go deeper. Everything I had ever published in the *IKC* was at least twice as good as my original submission, because of Bob's pushing.[1] But this time (for reasons that I needn't burden any of you with), I didn't allow myself to be pushed. That essay, my final contribution to the series that Bob had (in a very real sense) trusted me with in an increasingly intimate way, as I look back at it now, is clearly an unfinished project, unworthy of his faith in me.

That fact has haunted me ever since. On the occasion of being invited to be the respondent to this session, however, something happened. It was just a few weeks ago, as I was driving home from work and thinking about what I would (or wanted to) say in this response, having only the session title, and the titles of five papers to go on, and then it hit me: I want to do right vis-à-vis that final push; I want to finish that thought that Bob was pushing me to finish so many years ago—and I think that I now know how. I don't know how to define a "capability-communication," generically, but I think I have an example, probably the prime example. And I'm embarrassed to admit that what I'm about to say is something that I had already said, not even a year before I wrote that essay on the lecture notes, in a review of Merold Westphal's *Levinas and Kierkegaard in Dialogue*. What follows is the lone extended quotation from the book in the entire review, where Westphal is discussing the challenge posed, by Kierkegaard, for Levinas:

> Only by being loved do we develop the capacity to love, and Kierkegaard's God is fully personal enough for his answer to be 'We love because he first loved us' (I John 4:19).

---

[1] Of course, the various members of the IKC Advisory Committee who read and commented on my submissions are also due an expression of deep gratitude—but Bob was always the messenger, effectively communicating to me what needed to be communicated, and how.

> He gives us a moral transcription of God as *mysterium tremendum et fascinans*. God is *mysterium* by remaining hidden even within the piety of hidden inwardness, *tremendum* by commanding the subordination of self-love to neighbor love, and *fascinans* by being the fountain of forgiving love that gives us both our own sense of worth and our capacity to love others. Levinas' God is the *mysterium tremendum*; but where is the *fascinans* in the Good that gives no goods but only compels to goodness? When the command to love is unaccompanied by the love that enables obedience to the command, is this not a recipe for despair and even cynicism? (Westphal, *Levinas in Kierkegaard in Dialogue*, 72).

Love. Love is a capability that can be communicated. I am enabled to love (rendered capable of loving), by being loved. But I cannot truly love another, until I am loved. And others cannot truly love me until they are similarly enabled. And...etc., etc., etc., *ad infinitum*. Where, or rather how, does one begin (to begin), in this regard? This question, or something very like it, seems very much at the heart of all five of the preceding papers. And as the drafts from our authors/presenters began to trickle into my inbox, and especially once the last one arrived, something crystalized in my mind: the real problem is not what I used to think it was. The real problem is not that I am unwilling to love. The real problem is that I am unwilling to be loved—to be loved, not for the person that I am, or the person that I have become, or the *persona* that I project, but really and truly (i.e., unconditionally) loved. This may sound strange, and it should, because it's true. And this realization was not an epiphany of genius, no, it was cultivated in me, by others—and by others, *nota bene*, engaged in the decidedly political activity of debating the relative merits and demerits of ferreting political insights out of Kierkegaard's work, inspired by a single individual by the name of Robert L. Perkins.

It's amazing. Bob is still pushing me (and still pushing me to radically reconsider what I understand "being political" to mean). And Sylvia is still encouraging and inspiring me—God only knows why (or maybe he doesn't). I'd like very much to thank Bob (and Sylvia) for all this, but they would be the first to insist that such an expression of gratitude was radically misdirected. So, instead, I'll thank God, for Bob, and for Sylvia—and for John, Marilyn, Steve, George, and Lee (being pulled in five different directions was a great workout). And then I'll end this, my shtick, with the following: "Thus far, our authors/presenters can lead us. We invite our readers to learn what they can here, and then to become our teachers."[2]

[2] Robert L. Perkins (in every Introduction to every volume of the IKC).

Note on Contributors

JOHN DAVENPORT is Professor of Philosophy and Director of Peace & Justice Studies (2014-17) at Fordham University. He is the author of several books and many articles on Kierkegaard.

M.G. PIETY is Professor of Philosophy at Drexel University. She is the author of two books and many articles on Kierkegaard and the translator of his *Philosophical Crumbs and Repetition* (Oxford, 2009).

C. STEPHEN EVANS is University Professor of Philosophy and Humanities, director of the Baylor Center for Christian Philosophy, Distinguished Senior Fellow in the Institute for Studies of Religion at Baylor University, and a Professorial Fellow at the University of St. Andrews and at Australian Catholic University. He is the author of numerous books and articles on Kierkegaard.

GEORGE PATTISON is Professor of Divinity at the University of Glasgow. Previously he was Lady Margaret Professor of Divinity at the University of Oxford and Dean of the Chapel at King's College, Cambridge. He is the author of several books and many articles on Kierkegaard.

LEE C. BARRETT is the Mary B. and Henry P. Stager Professor of Theology at Lancaster Theological Seminary. He is the author of *Eros and Self-Emptying: The Intersections of Augustine and Kierkegaard* (Eerdmans, 2013) and *Kierkegaard* (Abingdon, 2010).

CHRISTOPHER A. P. NELSON is Professor of Philosophy at South Texas College. He was a frequent contributor to and evaluator for the *International Kierkegaard Commentary* series.

SHERIDAN HOUGH is Professor of Philosophy at the College of Charleston. She is the current President of the Søren Kierkegaard Society of North America and the author of *Kierkegaard's Dancing Tax Collector: Faith, Finitude, and Silence* (Oxford, 2015).

SYLVIA WALSH PERKINS taught at Emory University and Clark College in Atlanta, GA, and at Stetson University in DeLand, Florida. She is the author of several books on Kierkegaard and the translator of his *Fear and Trembling* (Cambridge, 2006) and *Discourses at the Communion on Fridays* (Indiana, 2011).

Select Bibliography

Allen, Julie K. "Orla Lehmann: Kierkegaard's Political Alter-Ego?" In *Kierkegaard and His Danish Contemporaries, Tome I: Philosophy, Politics and Social Theory*. Ed. by Jon Stewart. Farnham: Ashgate, 2009. 85-100.

Assiter, Alison. *Kierkegaard, Metaphysics and Political Theory*. London: Continuum, 2009.

Avanessian, Armen and Sophie Wennerscheid, eds. *Kierkegaard and Political Theory: Religion, Aesthetics, Politics and the Intervention of the Single Individual.* Copenhagen: Museum Tusculanum Press, 2014.

Backhouse, Stephen. *Kierkegaard's Critique of Christian Nationalism.* Oxford: Oxford University Press, 2011.

Barrett III, Lee C. "The Neighbor's Material and Social Well-Being in Kierkegaard's *Works of Love:* Does It Matter?" In *International Kierkegaard Commentary: 'Works of Love,'* Vol. 16. Ed. by Robert L. Perkins. Macon, GA: Mercer University Press, 1999. 137-65.

Bellinger, Charles K. "Toward a Kierkegaardian Understanding of Hitler, Stalin, and the Cold War." In *Foundatiions of Kierkegaard's Vision of Community*. Ed. by George B. Connell and C. Stephen Evans. London: Humanities Press, 1992. 218-30.

________________. *The Genealogy of Violence: Reflections on Creation, Freedom, and Evil.* Oxford: Oxford University Press, 2001.

_______________. *The Unrepentant Crowd: Søren Kierkegaard and Ernest Becker on the Roots of Political Violence.* www.createspace.com, 2016.

Best, Steven and Douglas Kellner. "Modernity, Mass Society, and the Media: Reflections on the *Corsair* Affair." In *International Kierkegaard Commentary: The Corsair Affair,* Vol. 13. Ed. by Robert L. Perkins, Macon, GA: Mercer University Press, 1990. 23–61.

Burns, Michael O'Neill. *Kierkegaard and the Matter of Philosophy: A Fractured Dialectic.* London and New York: Rowman and Littlefield, 2015.

Connell, George B. and C. Stephen Evans, eds. *Foundations of Kierkegaard's Vision of Community: Religion, Ethics, and Politics in Kierkegaard.* London: Humanities Press, 1992.

Dooley, Mark. "Risking Responsibility: a Politics of the Ėmigré." In *Kierkegaard: The Self in Society.* Ed. by George Pattison and Steven Shakespeare. Houndmills, Basingstoke, Hampshire and London: Macmillan, 1998. 139-55.

____________. "The Politics of Exodus: Derrida, Kierkegaard, and Levinas on 'Hospitality.'" In *International Kierkegaard Commentary: Works of Love.* Ed. by Robert L. Perkins. Macon, GA: Mercer University Press, 1999. 167-92.

____________. *The Politics of Exodus: Kierkegaard's Ethics of Responsibility.* New York: Fordham University Press, 2001.

Fletcher, David Bruce. *Social and Political Perspectives in the Thought of Søren Kierkegaard.* Washington, DC: University Press of America, 1982.

Gould, Rebecca. "Laws, Exceptions, Norms: Kierkegaard, Schmitt and Benjamin on the Exception." *Telos,* Vol. 162 (2013), 1-19.

Hyde, J. Keith. *Concepts of Power in Kierkegaard and Nietzsche.* Farnham, UK and Burlington, VT: Ashgate, 2010.

Kirmmse, Bruce H. *Kierkegaard in Golden Age Denmark.* Bloomington & Indianapolis: Indiana University Press, 1990.

______________. "'This Disastrous Confounding of Politics and Christianity': Kierkegaard's Open Letter of 1851." In *International Kierkegaard Commentary: The Corsair Affair,* Vol. 13. Ed. by Robert L. Perkins. Macon, GA: Mercer University Press, 1990. 179-84.

______________. "Call Me Ishmael—Call Everybody Ishmael: Kierkegaard on the Coming-of-Age Crisis of Modern Times." In *Foundations of Kierkegaard's Vision of Community.* Ed. by George B. Connell and C. Stephen Evans. London: Humanities Press, 1992. 161-82.

______________. "Kierkegaard and 1848." *History of European Ideas* 20, 1995: 167-75.

______________. "On Authority and Revolution: Kierkegaard's Road to Politics." In *Kierkegaard Revisited.* Ed. by Niels Jørgen Cappelørn and Jon Stewart. Berlin and New York: Walter de Gruyter, 1997. 254-73.

Koch, Carl Henrik, "Frederik Christian Sibbern: 'the lovable, remarkable thinker, Councilor Sibbern' and 'the political Simple-Peter Sibbern.'" In *Kierkegaard and His Danish Contemporaries, Tome I: Philosophy, Politics and Social Theory.* Ed. by Jon Stewart. Farnham, UK and Burlington, VT: Ashgate, 2009. 229-60.

Lappano, David. *Søren Kierkegaard's Theology of Encounter: An Edifying and Polemical Life.* Oxford: Oxford University Press, 2017.

Matuštik, Martin J. *Postnational Identity: Critical Theory and Existential Philosophy in Habermas, Kierkegaard, and Havel.* New York: Guilford Press, 1993.

______________. "Kierkegaard as Socio-Political Thinker and Activist." In *Man and World 27/2.* (April, 1994): 211-24.

———————. "Kierkegaard's Radical Existential Praxis, or: Why the Individual Defies Liberal, Communitarian, and Postmodern Categories." In *Kierkegaard in Post/Modernity*. Ed. by Martin J Matuštik and Merold Westphal. Bloomington and Indianapolis: Indiana University Press, 1995. 239-64.

Műller, Paul. "Kierkegaard som social og politisk tænker." In *Kierkegaardiana XIII.* Ed. by N. J. Cappelørn, Helge Hultberg, and Poul Lűbcke. København: C. A. Reitzels Forlag, 1984. 122-27.

Nicoletti, Michele. "Politics and Religion in Kierkegaard's Thought: Secularization and the Martyr." In *Foundations of Kierkegaard's Vision of Community.* Ed. by George B. Connell and C. Stephen Evans. London: Humanities Press, 1992. 183-95.

Opitz, Andrew M. "Kierkegaard, Gramsci, and the Politics of Irony and Sarcasm." *Comparative Literature* 64:3 (2012): 270-85.

Pattison, George and Steven Shakespeare, eds. *Kierkegaard: The Self in Society.* Houndmills, Basingstoke, Hampshire and London: Macmillan, 1998.

Perkins, Robert L. "Kierkegaard's Anti-Climacus in His Social and Political Environment." In *International Kierkegaard Commentary: 'Practice in Christianity.'* Vol. 20. Macon, GA: Mercer University Press, 2004. 275-302.

———————. "Upbuilding as a Propaedeutic for Justice." In *International Kierkegaard Commentary: 'Eighteen Upbuilding Discourses.'* Vol. 5. Macon, GA: Mercer University Press, 2003. 325-56.

———————. "Power, Politics, and Media Critique: Kierkegaard's First Brush with the Public Press." In *International Kierkegaard Commentary: 'Early Polemical Writings.'* Vol. 1. Macon: GA: Mercer University Press, 1999. 27-44.

———————. "Climacan Politics: Person and Polis in Kierkegaard's *Postscript.*" In *International Kierkegaard Commentary: 'Concluding Unscientific Postscript.'* Vol. 12. Macon, GA: Mercer University Press, 1997. 33-52. Reprinted in *Kierkegaard: The Self in*

Society. Ed. by George Pattison and Steven Shakespeare. Houndmills, Basingstoke, Hampshire and London: Macmillan, 1998. 43-53.

_____________. "Envy as Personal Phenomenon and as Politics." In *International Kierkegaard Commentary: 'Two Ages.'* Vol.14. Macon, GA: Mercer University Press, 1984. 107-32.

_____________. "The Authoritarian Symbiosis of Church and Crown in Kierkegaard's Attack on Christendom." In *Anthropology and Authority: Essays on Søren Kierkegaard.* Ed. by Paul Houe, Gordon D. Marino, and Sven Hakon Rossel. Atlanta and Amsterdam: Rodopi, 2000. 137-43.

_____________. "Language, Social Reality, and Resistance in the Age of Kierkegaard's Review of *Two Ages*." In *Kierkegaard Studies Yearbook 1999.* Ed. by Niels Jørgen Cappelørn and Hermann Deuser. Berlin: Walter de Gruyter, 1999. 165-81.

_____________. "Kierkegaard's Social Thought in the Post Cold War World." In *Kierkegaard Revisited.* Kierkegaard Monograph Series, No. 1. Ed. by Niels Jørgen Cappelørn. Berlin and New York: Walter de Gruyter, 1997. 139-55.

_____________. "The Politics of Existence: Buber and Kierkegaard." In *Kierkegaard in Post/Modernity.* Ed. by Martin J. Matuštik and Merold Westphal. Bloomington, IN: Indiana University Press, 1995. 167-80.

_____________. "Kierkegaard's Critique of the Bourgeois State." *Inquiry*, Vol. 27 (1984): 207-18.

Ryan, Bartholomew, ed. *Kierkegaard's Indirect Politics: Interludes with Lukács, Schmitt, Benjamin, and Adorno.* Rodopi: Amsterdam and New York, *2014.*

Simmons, J. Aaron. *God and the Other: Ethics and Politics After the Theological Turn.* Bloomington: Indiana University Press, 2011.

Simmons, J. Aaron and David Wood, eds. *Kierkegaard and Levinas: Ethics, Politics, and Religion.* Bloomington: Indiana University Press, 2008.

Smith, Graham M. *Friendship & the Political: Kierkegaard, Nietzsche, Schmitt.* Imprint–Academic, 2011.

_______________. "Kierkegaard From the Point of View of the Political." *History of European Ideas,* Vol. 31/1 (2005): 35-60.

Sirvent, Roberto and Silas Morgan, eds. *Kierkegaard and Political Theology.* Eugene, OR: Pickwick Publications, 2018.

Stewart, Jon, ed. *Kierkegaard and His Danish Contemporaries, Tome I: Philosophy, Politics, and Social Theory.* Farnham: Ashgate, 2009.

__________, ed. *Kierkegaard's Influence on Social-Political Thought.* Farnham: Ashgate, 2011.

Stocker, Barry. *Kierkegaard on Politics.* Houndmills, Blasingstoke, Hampshire: Palgrave MacMillan, 2014.

Surman, Darren. *Kierkegaard and the Political Theory of Love: Love is a Revolution.* Routledge, 2018.

Tilley, J. Michael. "Kierkegaard's Attempt at Social Philosophy: An Examination of Kierkegaard's Relationship to Karl Bayer." In *Kierkegaard and His German Contemporaries, Tome I: Philosophy.* Ed. by Jon Stewart. Farnham: Ashgate, 2007. 17-24.

_______________. "Interpersonal Relationships and Community in Kierkegaard's Thought." Ph. D. Diss. University of Kentucky, 2008.

_____________ "Ditlev Gothard Monrad: Kierkegaard on Politics, the Liberal Movement, and the Danish Constitution." In *Kierkegaard and His Danish Contemporaries, Tome I: Philosophy, Politics, and Social Theory.* Ed. Jon Stewart. Farnham: Ashgate, 2009. 169-77.

_____________. "J. L. A. Koldurup-Rosenvinge: Kierkegaard on Walking away from Politics." In *Kierkegaard and His Danish Contemporaries, Tome I: Philosophy, Politics, and Social Theory.* Ed. John Stewart. Farnham, Ashgate, 2009. 77-83.

Westphal, Merold. "Kierkegaard's Politics." *Thought* 55:218 (1980): 320—32.

______________. *Kierkegaard's Critique of Reason and Society.* University Park: The Pennsylvania State University Press, 1991.

_____________. "Society, Politics, and Modernity," In *The Oxford Handbook of Kierkegaard.* Ed. by John Lippitt and George Pattison. Oxford: Oxford University Press, 2013. 309-27.

Index